TETON CLASSICS

ii

TETON CLASSICS

SELECTED CLIMBS IN GRAND TETON NATIONAL PARK

RICHARD ROSSITER

CHOCKSTONE PRESS, INC.
Evergreen, Colorado
1991

Cover photos by Richard Rossiter: (front) Joyce Rossiter on the CMC Route, Mount Moran, the West Horn in the background.
All uncredited photos by the author.
All artwork and graphics are original and by the author.

ISBN 0-934641-13-7

Published and distributed by
Chockstone Press, Inc.
Post Office Box 3505
Evergreen, Colorado 80439

Warning

This is only a guidebook. It is merely a composite of opinions from many sources on the whereabouts and difficulties of the climbing routes included. It is not an instruction book on mountaineering technique or a substitute for the user's judgement. Climbing the routes described in this book is a high risk activity and the user of this guide to those routes either assumes full responsibility for his or her safety or should not use this book.

Acknowledgements

THE ROUTE DESCRIPTIONS in this book are based on the author's personal experience in the Tetons and on the corroboration of several other friends and associates. For lending their assistance and expertise, I would like to thank and recognize Paul Gagner, Tim Hogan, Ted Karasote, and the Teton ranger staff at Jenny Lake. In addition. Sharlene Milligan, and others of the Grand Teton Natural History Association, provided invaluable input as the project progressed.

Historical information including names and dates of first ascents is drawn from *Mountaineering in the Tetons 1898 to 1940* by Fritiof Fryxell, various annums of the *American Alpine Journal,* and *A Climber's Guide to the Teton Range* by Leigh Ortenburger.

Table of

Contents

South Buttress Right, pitch three, Mount Moran

Introduction

MY FIRST VIEW OF THE TETONS came in the spring of 1968. While on leave from the army, I drove my Volkswagen bug across the continent from the coast of South Carolina to the Pacific Northwest. I went through every scenic spot that I could find – and still have time to visit my family – before taking an overseas assignment with Special Forces. In early June, against an outlandish headwind, my little VW sputtered and struggled westward up the long incline toward Togwotee Pass. The scenery was wholly new and magnificent and kindled in me a mounting anticipation for this unknown mountain range upon which I was soon to gaze. I had been to Mount Rainier, the Olympic Mountains, Yosemite, and, on this trip, the Great Smokies, but as I crossed the divide, a surpassing and ethereal vista opened before me. I felt as though I had entered Valhalla. I pulled over, got out of the car, and stared in wonderment. Before me, the mighty, jagged Tetons thrust upward into a storm-ripped sky. Great purple clouds were lifting from the dark summits, trailing long tendrils of snow and spindrift, while shafts of golden light poured from behind onto the forests and lakes. I stood there in the wind for a long time and took a few pictures. Eventually, I drove down into Jackson Hole for the night, and though I did not stay to explore and climb, that scene was etched indelibly into my consciousness. I knew I would return.

Now, more than twenty years have passed since I made that journey and I have come back to the Tetons many times, to climb the great routes and wander in the high places. Though the valleys, lakes, and peaks have become familiar, their mystique is not lost to me. Never have I driven across the expansive flats of Jackson Hole without being thrilled by the rugged profile and awesome relief of these wonderful mountains, nor has any outing, even a climb repeated, been less than exhilarating.

Could one actually tire of such things? Getting acquainted with the Tetons is not, after all, the business of a few vacations, but the passion of a lifetime – and still, there will be lakes unseen, ridges not climbed, and grand adventures awaiting.

•

ONE OF THE DISTINGUISHING characteristics of the Teton Range is that, from the east, it rises very abruptly, without the typical intermediary of foothills. The lower slopes of the range, cloaked in trees and jewel-like lakes, simply fall away beneath several thousand feet of sheer rock, glaciers, and hanging snowfields that stand in stark contrast to the arid, sage-dotted plains of Jackson Hole. The highest peak in the range, the Grand Teton, soars 7000 feet above the floor of a valley that was once the haunt of Indians and mountain men. Adding to the sense of drama, most of the summits are fairly narrow, with all the highest peaks lined up along the western margin of the flat valley. The ultimate effect is that of a great, impregnable wall of crags like the Ered Nimrais in J.R.R. Tolkien's trilogy, the Lord of the Rings. Though there are other very dramatic mountain ranges in this part of the world, such as the Picket Range in the North Cascades, none have the isolation and vertical relief, not to mention ease of access, of the Tetons.

From a climber's perspective, the Tetons offer a wide range of compelling options in an incomparable alpine setting. The routes vary from enjoyable scrambles, such as the East Face of Teewinot, to high-angle rock masterpieces, like the South Buttress Right on Mount Moran. Then, there are the great alpine classics, such as the Black Ice Couloir on the Grand Teton and sweeping snow climbs like the Glacier Route on the Middle Teton. During the winter, even the easiest routes become challenging. One can expect snow and ice to cover everything, and high winds and extreme cold will add to the danger and excitement. The Owen-Spalding route on the Grand Teton is one of the more popular winter outings. Several waterfalls form up, including Raven Crack and Rimrock Lake Outlet in Death Canyon, and provide excellent, steep ice climbs. As for approaches, most of the climbs listed in this book can be done in a single day and likely have been by very fit and capable athletes. For the average party, approaches to climbs will range from one hour to a full day and, in some cases, may be facilitated by tour boat or canoe. The hard work of reaching the climbs is, however, offset by the grandeur of the terrain, the uplifting alpine atmosphere, and, of course, the great climbing.

For those accustomed to such lowland haunts as Smith Rock and Eldorado Canyon – to whom Teton approaches might seem desperately long, the holds on the rock too large, and the need for gear beyond quickdraws an unwieldy burden – a limestone "sport crag" (whoa!) has been developed within the park. Just north of Moose Junction on the east side of Highway 191, one will find a small, gray rock outcrop on the north shoulder of Blacktail Butte. There are about a dozen bolted climbs on the very steep southwest face that range in difficulty from 9 to 13a. A topo of this 60-foot-high crag can be had at no charge from Teton Mountaineering, an outdoor shop in Jackson Hole. While there, also inquire about the Hoback Shield.

Teton rock generally is quite solid, and for the most part has good cracks. Contrary to the notion of many climbers, the peaks do not consist entirely of granite. Precambrian gneiss and schist form the core of the range; only the highest peaks from Buck Mountain to Leigh Canyon are composed of a preponderance of granite. Even within the granite, there are large, angular masses or blocks of the more ancient gneiss, so that on a single climb one usually will encounter more than one type of rock. Further, a labyrinth of granite and pegmatite dikes runs throughout the range, with massive, vertical dikes of black diabase distinguishing several of the main peaks. Teton rock provides excellent climbing with abundant holds and reasonable protection. In the case of incipient cracks or blank areas where nuts are difficult or impossible to place, one happily finds fixed pins and an occasional bolt. Bear in mind, however, that fixed gear – especially pitons – come loose with time and should be backed up with other protection when possible.

On Equipment

In the Tetons, appropriate climbing hardware can vary drastically from one route to another, and for any one of them, what a climber chooses to bring mostly is a matter of taste and style. There is, however – at least in terms of crack width – a general grouping of devices that most parties would want to carry on a given route. Thus, a "standard Teton rack" might consist of the following pieces:

- A set of RPs
- Wired stoppers up to one inch
- 3 or 4 TCUs
- 2 or 3 Hexs or Tri-cams
- Various camming devices up to three inches (#4 Friend)
- 6 or 7 quick draws

- 5 or 6 runners long enough to wear over the shoulder
- 7 or 8 unoccupied carabiners (typically with the runners)
- Double 9 mm X 165-foot ropes are recommended.

Specific equipment suggestions are given with some route descriptions.

NOTE: Certain equipment brand names sometimes are given. This is not to express a prejudice against other manufacturers, but because certain brands are so often used that they serve as a standard of measurement. For example, it is easier to describe the maximum width of a crack in terms of a #3 Friend rather than inches simply because a climber is more likely to carry a #3 Friend than a ruler. I am, emphatically, not suggesting that the named device is in any way superior to similar devices of a different manufacture.

Ratings

The system used in this book for rating difficulty is a descendant of the so-called Yosemite decimal system, which in turn, is a descendant of one developed at Tahquitz Rock and introduced by the Sierra Club in 1937. This was based on the German Welzenbach grades, which divided terrain difficulty into six classes according to the techniques and equipment one would typically employ. Class one, for example, was merely off-trail hiking. Class three was harder, requiring the frequent use of hands and basic free climbing techniques. Class five was roped free climbing (where the average party would place gear for safety), and class six was direct aid (where gear placed in the rock was relied upon for support).

By the 1950s, rock climbing had evolved to the point where six classes of difficulty, from walking uphill to direct aid, were a bit too broad, especially since the major focus was on class five climbing. Thus, class five was subdivided into 10 units and written as 5.0 through 5.9, while class six was divided into five units and written as A1 through A5. This worked well enough until a climb harder than 5.9 was completed, which necessitated the numerical absurdity of 5.10 or the development of a new rating system. As we all know, American climbers settled for the former.

By the early 1970s, free climbing was sufficiently well developed in Yosemite that the subdivisions a, b, c, and d were added to grades 5.10 and harder, further complicating an illogical system that, by comparison, makes inches, feet, and yards look rather well thought out. Though most of us are accustomed to it, the "decimal system" is a dinosaur looking for a place to die, and I would like to give it an opportunity to do so with this book.

If we eliminate the original six classes of the Welzenbach system and drop the decimal point, we are left with an open-ended series of whole numbers from 0 to 14 (onward if needed) that represents all levels of roped free climbing and does not require reassignment of ratings to existing routes. 5.4 simply becomes 4, 5.9+ becomes 9+, and 5.12c becomes 12c. The letter grades a, b, c, and d, and perhaps the + are useful and can be applied as before. Regarding easier terrain, it is enough to say that it is a walk (hands not needed) or a scramble (hands used for balance) and need not be further subdivided into numerical categories. Thus, we have a logical, streamlined system, the

North Face of the Grand

Paul Gagner photo

application of which requires very little adjustment and is easily comprehended by the uninitiated. The Roman numerals for overall difficulty are employed in the customary manner.

[At best, these ratings represent the concensus of climbers, that is to say, they are opinion and nothing more. It is essential to remember that this is only a guide to the routes; in the end, it is your skill and judgement that will keep you alive on the rocks. **If you do not fully understand the rating system described above, do not use this book.**]

Environmental Considerations

It goes without saying that the magnificent landscape and fragile ecosystem of the Tetons is a precious heritage and deserves our deepest respect, appreciation, and best effort toward preservation. Unlike parks in a more urban setting, where disposable diapers, food containers, and Kleenex lurk behind every bush, the Tetons are refreshingly clean and well-kept; this may be attributed to a relatively conscious and well-educated visitor population and enthusiastic park staff. As for the sport of climbing, perhaps the greatest environmental impact is from off-trail foot traffic. There is the occasional food wrapper, bit of tape, and toilet paper showing from under rocks – even cigarette butts stuffed into cracks – but it is the long-term wear and tear of feet, especially those clad in mountain boots, that leave lasting scars on the range.

To preserve the natural beauty and ecological integrity of our climbing environment, a few suggestions are offered. Deposit solid human waste away from camps and paths of approach. Do not cover it with a rock, but leave it exposed to the elements, where it will deteriorate more quickly. In the lower forests, it can be buried. Carry used toilet paper out in a plastic bag, or wipe with a stick or Douglas fir cone. Do not leave man-made riff-raff lying about. If you pack it in, pack it out. Take care to preserve trees and other plants on approaches and climbs. Use trails and footpaths where they have been developed, and demonstrate human evolution by removing obstructions, stacking loose rocks along the trail sides, and picking up trash. When hiking across tundra, follow footpaths or step on rocks to avoid crushing the fragile plantlife.

Fires are allowed only at campsites with firegrates. It is best to use portable campstoves for all cooking. Do not feed or interfere with birds and animals. Bears are natural scavengers; they will tear into and eat anything that smells remotely like food. It is essential to hang food 10 feet or more above the ground. Some campsites have metal poles with hooks for this purpose. In other cases, food should be slung from tree limbs so that it is six feet from the tree and ten to twelve feet off the ground (see *Teewinot,* a park tabloid, for instructions). Check with the National Park Service for other suggestions and regulations.

Weather and Snow Conditions

Climbing in the Tetons is done primarily from late June through September. During this period, one can expect comfortable to hot daytime temperatures, sunny mornings, and afternoon thundershowers. Up until mid-July, nearly every peak climb will require an ice axe and mountain boots – at least for the approach to specific rock features. Rapid descents can be made via glissade. From late July through August, the weather usually is hot during the day and many climbs can be done without any snow travel. There also is, typically, an auspicious period of two or three weeks in late July or August distinguished by a lack of afternoon thunderstorms. Temperatures will cool some in September, but the climbs are usually still dry. By October, the first serious snows may come, but good climbing still can be had, especially on south-facing features. In November, it gets cold and the winter ice climbs begin to form up. Spring is avalanche time in the Tetons. Check with the rangers for conditions.

Visitor Facilities and Services

Though there is a campground and visitor center at Colter Bay, climbers primarily will be interested in the visitor center at Moose and the rustic ranger station at Jenny Lake. Nearly all climbing activity begins and ends at these locations, not only for their strategic proximity to the main peaks, but because the National Park Service requires climbers to register in person for every outing. One also must check in upon return. Whereas this may seem an unnecessary procedure to some, it serves good purpose, not the least of which is getting help if things go awry on your climb. The rangers at Jenny Lake all are experienced Teton climbers and have a wealth of practical information for the asking. Guide books and maps are available at both locations.

To reach Moose and Jenny Lake from Highway 191 (the main road that runs north and south through the plains of Jackson Hole), turn west at Moose Junction onto the Teton Park Road. The first turn on the right leads to Dornan's, where one finds a climbing shop (mountain bike rental), grocery store (canoe rental), liquor store, bar/lounge, gas station and other conveniences. Continuing west on the Teton Park Road, one will encounter the Moose Visitor Center on the right and Moose Village stores on the left (with post office). Next, one passes through an entrance station, where a fee is required. Pick up a free park map and a copy of Teewinot, a park tabloid with much useful information. Follow the road as it bends around to head north and after about eight super-scenic miles turn left at South Jenny Lake Junction. Another half-mile or so brings one to the quaint Jenny Lake complex. The most strategic campground for climbers is at Jenny Lake (see also Gros Ventre and Signal Mountain Campgrounds). There are many other facilities inside the park –

and in the town of Jackson – including good restaurants, laundromats, outdoor shops, and way too much to list here. Stop at the Jackson Chamber of Commerce for a map of town and list of services.

How to Use this Book

This book is intended for the experienced climber; it is not a manual of instruction, but a guide to the routes. It assumes that the reader is already proficient in the placement of climbing hardware, the use of a rope, and has climbed before in the mountains. At least two climbing schools are available in the park for those who seek instruction or the service of a guide. Wheras this book contains much useful information, it cannot take the place of skill and good judgement. Take care inplanning an ascent. Be sure to have proper gear and clothing. Allow adequate time to complete a route – an unplanned bivouac canbe disastrous. Teton weather can deteriorate rapidly, and a bright, sunny day can turn into a violent storm. Rockfall can occur on any route at any time. Regardless of experience, if the situation in which you find yourself does not look good, consider retreat. You can always return another day.

Topo Symbols

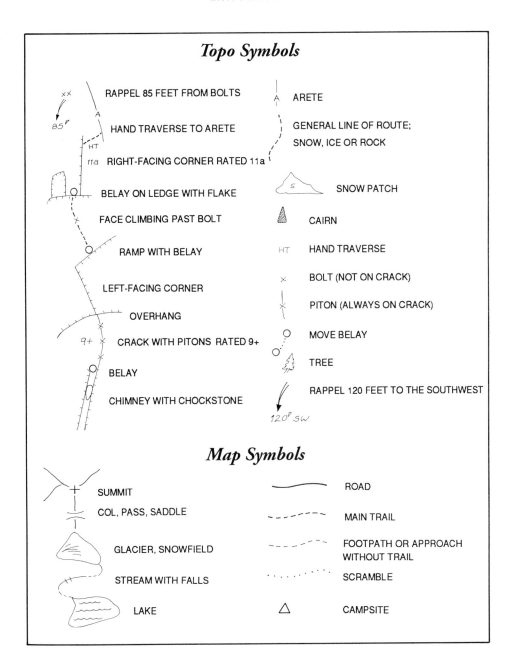

RAPPEL 85 FEET FROM BOLTS

HAND TRAVERSE TO ARETE

RIGHT-FACING CORNER RATED 11a

BELAY ON LEDGE WITH FLAKE

FACE CLIMBING PAST BOLT

RAMP WITH BELAY

LEFT-FACING CORNER

OVERHANG

CRACK WITH PITONS RATED 9+

BELAY

CHIMNEY WITH CHOCKSTONE

ARETE

GENERAL LINE OF ROUTE;
SNOW, ICE OR ROCK

SNOW PATCH

CAIRN

HAND TRAVERSE

BOLT (NOT ON CRACK)

PITON (ALWAYS ON CRACK)

MOVE BELAY

TREE

RAPPEL 120 FEET TO THE SOUTHWEST

Map Symbols

SUMMIT

COL, PASS, SADDLE

GLACIER, SNOWFIELD

STREAM WITH FALLS

LAKE

ROAD

MAIN TRAIL

FOOTPATH OR APPROACH
WITHOUT TRAIL

SCRAMBLE

CAMPSITE

Cathedral Rock

DEATH CANYON IS THE SECOND major drainage up from the south boundary of Grand Teton National Park. This spectacular glacier-carved valley is one of the most popular approaches to the Teton Crest Trail and, along with great hiking, sports some of the best crag climbing in the entire range. In winter, the canyon provides a fine ski tour and has two excellent ice climbs on the north face of Prospectors Mountain. The main climbing attraction, however, is Cathedral Rock, the 1000-foot-high south buttress of Point 10,552. This beautiful feature, more accurately a "wall" than a "rock," looms up dramatically on the north as one hikes into the narrows of Death Canyon. There are several good routes on this very steep wall, two of which – THE SNAZ and CAVEAT EMPTOR – have become indisputable Teton classics.

Approach. From Moose Junction, drive south on the Moose-Wilson Road. After several miles, turn right at a signed junction and drive to a parking area at the White Grass Ranger Station and the end of the road. The Death Canyon Trailhead is located here. This trail climbs gently to a scenic shoulder above Phelps Lake, then drops into the narrows of Death Canyon. After a level stretch in the forested valley bottom, the trail climbs steeply via eight switchbacks and passes directly beneath Cathedral Rock. A footpath that leads to the beginning of the routes climbs steeply back to the northeast from the eighth switchback. The beginning of this path is a

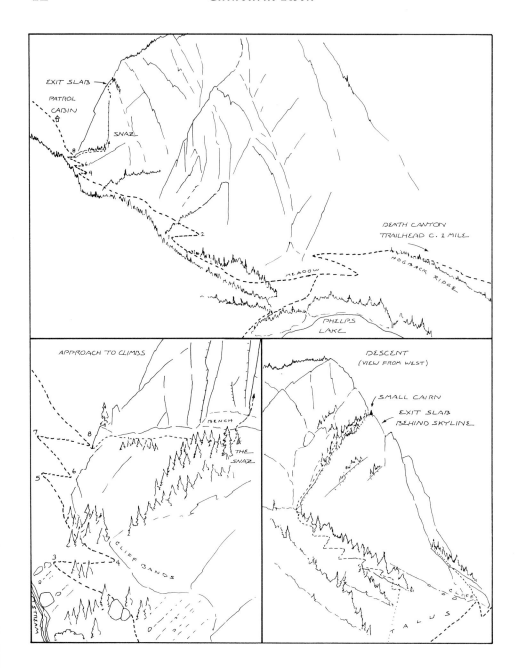

EXIT SLAB
PATROL CABIN
SNAZ

DEATH CANYON TRAILHEAD C. 1 MILE
HOGBACK RIDGE
MEADOW
PHELPS LAKE

APPROACH TO CLIMBS
BENCH
THE SNAZ
CLIFF BANDS
STREAM

DESCENT
(VIEW FROM WEST)
SMALL CAIRN
EXIT SLAB BEHIND SKYLINE
CLIFF
TALUS

steep scramble that is somewhat unpleasant to descend. Therefore, one may want to stash extraneous gear near the end of the downclimb, rather than bringing it up to the base of the wall.

The main trail levels off a short way beyond the eighth switchback and at 2.5 miles (from the trailhead) reaches a patrol cabin and a junction with the Alaska Basin Trail. Before heading up the climber's path, it is a good idea to walk up toward the junction to where the southwest side of the cliff can be viewed easily. The downclimb follows the forested ledge that begins on the right skyline and diagonals down and left across the face to the forested slope. From there, a path leads down through trees and talus to the Death Canyon Trail not far from the patrol cabin. The downclimb does not return to the base of the main wall. Thus, an extra circuit of the approach path can be avoided by leaving gear here. Remember to take precautions for bears.

The Snaz
Grade III 10a

ONE MAY WONDER, what exactly is a snaz? For an answer, we would have to ask Yvon Chouinard, who, with Mort Hempel, made the first ascent of this route on August 4, 1964. Fine steep rock, a warm southern exposure, and a relatively easy approach and descent combine to make THE SNAZ one of the most popular pure rock climbs in the Tetons. All of the belays are on good ledges and pitches two through seven now have fixed anchors with rappel rings. The protection is good on all pitches including variations. Rack up to 4 inches with extra pieces from one inch up. To find the beginning of the route, hike the climber's path to a large tree beneath an immense open book dihedral that runs up the center of the wall. Step up to the highest ground and belay at a slab beneath a small left-facing corner with a tree.

1. Climb up and right into the corner and work up to a broad grassy ledge (5). Run the rope out and belay beneath or just above a blocky overhang (6).
2. Work up a steep, not too clean, left-facing corner, move right and up to a belay at the bottom of another left-facing dihedral (7).
3. Follow the dihedral up through a wide slot and continue up to a good stance beneath an offwidth crack with a wedged block (7).

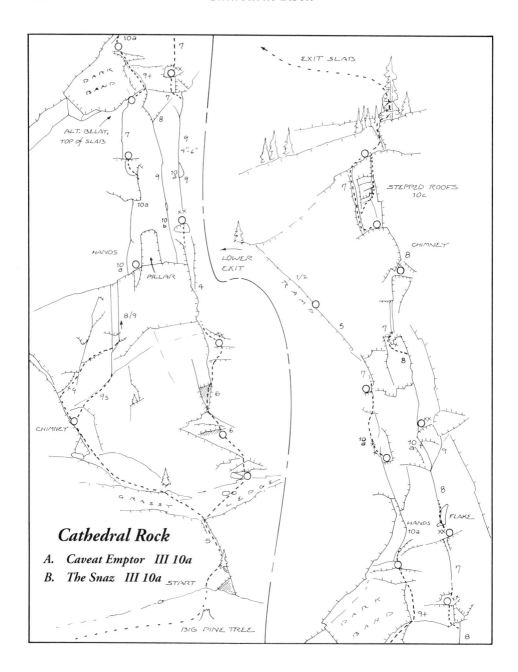

Cathedral Rock

A. **Caveat Emptor III 10a**
B. **The Snaz III 10a**

4. Now the climb gets going. Jam up around the right side of the block (9) and continue up the long, wide crack (8 or 9) to a roof that is turned on the left (8).

5. From the stance above the roof, climb an easy crack and corner to a ledge beneath a large detached flake (7).

6. This is a great pitch. Work up past a loose block and around the left side of the flake, continue up the fist crack (8), then jam and stem out a magnificent overhanging crack to yet another good ledge (10a). It is possible – but not recommended – to avoid the overhang by working around it on the right (9).

7. Work straight up a steep dihedral (7) for about 60 feet, traverse left to the far side of a hanging block (7),

The Snaz, seventh pitch

then work up through the roof, up short double cracks to a ledge (7), and up a crack on the right to a sloping ledge beneath an alcove.

8. Make tricky moves up into a bombay chimney (8) and follow it until it is possible to step left around an arête to a big ledge.

9. The traditional last pitch takes the double crack and chimney on the left to another ledge (7). For a more climactic, but well protected finish, undercling and lieback out the huge, stepped overhang on the right and arrive at the same belay ledge (10c).

Descent. In dry conditions, most parties unrope on the final belay ledge. Now, one must go up before going down. Scramble up the chimney above the belay (5) to a ledge with trees. Move right (east) to the largest tree and climb up onto a broad, smooth slab that is slippery when wet. The objective is to reach the higher, forested ledge. Climb straight up the slab to the ledge; or, more easily, climb up about 60 feet to a rounded ledge and follow this to the west for about 300 feet (no pro) until it is easy to gain the forested ledge. Now, hike west about 400 feet to a three-stone cairn. From here, a gully-and-chimney system cuts down across the southwest face of Cathedral Rock to the talus. A series of crude switchbacks (please use them) lead down through the trees to open talus, and a few hundred feet of boulder-hopping bring one to the level section of the trail above the eighth switchback. It is possible to royally screw up this descent, especially in the dark. It is, in fact, extremely dangerous to attempt this descent after nightfall. Best wait until morning when navigational errors can be rectified by rappelling from trees. One also may go west from the last belay of THE SNAZ or CAVEAT EMPTOR and descend along a lower series of ledges.

Caveat Emptor
Grade III 10a

THIS IS A LATIN IDIOM that means, "Let the buyer beware." That the climb deserves such an ominous name is subject to question, since it is probably the best rock climb in Death Canyon and is largely devoid of disappointments and unpleasant surprises. The line runs parallel and near to THE SNAZ on the left, but is harder and much more sustained in difficulty. The first ascent is credited to Jim Beyer and Buck Tilley who first climbed the route as it is described here in July, 1979, but a number of other people had climbed parts of the route previously. Rack up to 4 inches with extra pieces from one inch up.

1. Climb the initial pitch of THE SNAZ to get up onto the big, grassy ledge (5), then angle up and left on ramps and ledges (4) to the base of a left-leaning chimney.
2. Start up the chimney to a fixed pin, hand traverse right to a crack, and climb straight up (9) to a right-facing corner. Work up the corner, then angle right to belay on a ledge beside a large pillar.
3. To the left of the pillar, climb a beautiful finger crack up to a roof (10a). Turn the roof on the right (10a) and belay on a ledge after about 30 feet. It also is possible

to continue up a crack (7) and belay beneath a band of dark rock (165 feet overall).

4. Climb the crack (7) up to an overhang in an area of dark rock (possible belay on slab), make difficult moves up through the roof (10a), and belay across from the detached flake on the sixth pitch of THE SNAZ (90 feet).

5. Power up through the overhanging crack (10a) (possible belay on a small ledge), up through a left-facing corner and roof (9), and belay on a ledge that is below and right of some fixed protection (150 feet).

6. Move up and left about 10 feet to a fixed pin, straight up past a bashie (a bashed-in metal blob with a sling attached) (10a), back right to a left-facing corner, and up to a belay ledge (90 feet).

7. Climb an unprotected face (6), then follow a left-angling ramp to a ledge (150 feet).

8. Work up and left along easier terrain to the broad slab above THE SNAZ. To descend, climb up and left across the slab to the forested ledge, or work left. See descent for THE SNAZ above.

Caveat Emptor, pitch 2

Paul Gagner photo

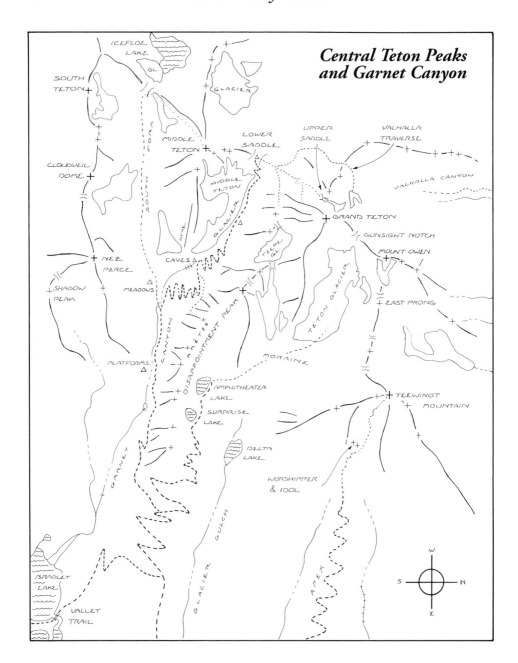

Central Teton Peaks and Garnet Canyon

The Grand Teton, Mount Owen, and Teewinot Mountain

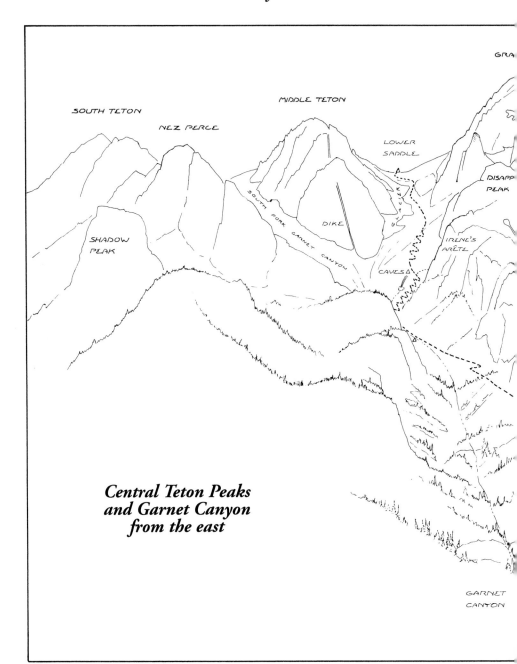

SOUTH TETON

NEZ PERCE

MIDDLE TETON

LOWER
SADDLE

GRA

DISAPP
PEAK

SHADOW
PEAK

SOUTH FORK GARNET CANYON

DIKE

GLACIER

IRENE'S
ARÊTE

CAVES

GARNET
CANYON

**Central Teton Peaks
and Garnet Canyon
from the east**

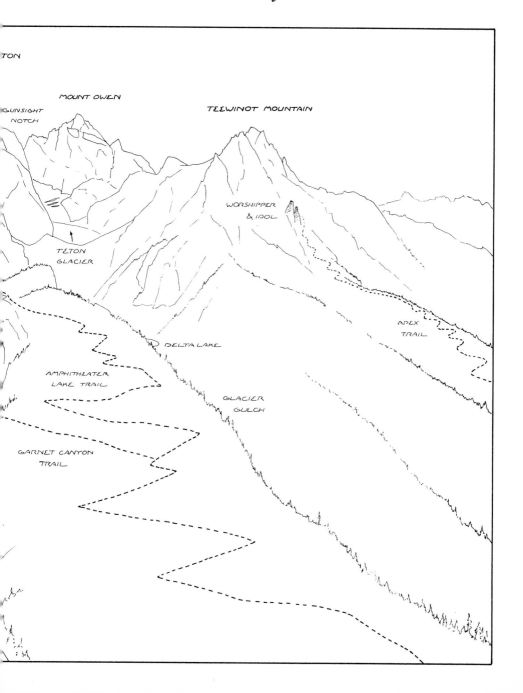

TON

GUNSIGHT
NOTCH

MOUNT OWEN

TEEWINOT MOUNTAIN

WORSHIPPER
& IDOL

TETON
GLACIER

APEX
TRAIL

DELTA LAKE

AMPHITHEATER
LAKE TRAIL

GLACIER
GULCH

GARNET CANYON
TRAIL

Disappointment Peak

As far as Teton summits are concerned, we could say that Disappointment Peak lives up to its name. With the loftiest peaks of the range towering above to the west, this stumpy wedge of rock attracts little attention from mountaineers and tourists. This is not to say that the view from the summit is dreary. It is, actually, sublime, and the ascent from Amphitheater Lake is a splendid alpine scramble – the same scramble, in fact, made by Phil Smith and Walter Harvey, who inadvertently bagged the first ascent of Disappointment Peak on August 20, 1925 in a thwarted attempt to climb the Grand Teton. In another, flatter place, this peak alone might justify a national park, but literally hidden against the mighty backdrop of the central Tetons, it goes almost completely unnoticed . . . except by rock climbers.

Disappointment Peak is situated immediately southeast of the Grand Teton and forms the divide between Glacier Gulch and Garnet Canyon. It has a very steep, 1000-foot northeast face that has seen some climbing activity, but the main attraction is the long row of south-facing arêtes and buttresses directly above the Garnet Canyon Trail. Due to their proximity, warm southern exposure, and high visibility to climbers approaching the Grand Teton, many routes have been done on these features. While some of these routes have fallen into obscurity, a few have withstood the test of time and have become popular. Of them all, a solitary route stands out, and has gained a wide reputation as one of the best rock climbs in all the

Tetons. Long before most climbers make their first journey to these mountains, they are aware of a route called IRENE'S ARETE.

Irene's Arête
Grade III   8 or 10a

AS ONE HIKES WESTWARD FROM the platforms in Garnet Canyon, an unusually sharp, clean fin of rock draws the eye from the other less well-formed features on the right skyline. This is IRENE'S ARETE, which was first climbed by John Dietschy and Irene Ortenburger on July 10, 1957. Though the route is not terribly difficult, the climbing is fairly sustained, the rock is beautiful, and unlike many other Teton outings, there are no dud pitches. Rack up to 3 inches. The more difficult "direct" variations are credited to Jim Olson and Mark Chapman, who climbed the arête on July 2, 1970.

Approach. Hike the Garnet Canyon Trail all the way to the last of the switchbacks (18) below Petzoldt's Caves. Continue west past the cliffband on the right, then, about 150 feet before reaching the top of Spalding Falls, turn right on a faint footpath that climbs steeply up scree to the north. Work back around to the top of the cliffband, where a broad, wooded ledge leads about 200 yards east to the base of IRENE'S ARETE. The initial grove of trees is a good place to leave extra gear. Just east of the grove, follow the ledge down around the foot of a small buttress, then scramble up the far side to a notch with a large pine tree. You now are directly beneath the objective. Turn north, then scramble up and left along ramps and short cliffs to a ledge that is just west of the continuous aspect of the arête. Belay here, or pull around onto the east side of the arête and belay atop a pedestal.

1. Climb discontinuous cracks up and right from the pedestal (7) and belay in a tiny alcove (100 feet).
2. Jam straight up a steep hand crack with fixed pins (8), and belay on a big ledge (100 feet). Move the belay north to the base of the next steep step in the arête.
3a. Climb about 10 feet just left of the crest, then pull around to the right into a marginal crack system (7). Work straight up in a dihedral of black rock, pull around to the left side of the crest, and jam another 30 feet up to a good ledge on the right side of the crest (7; 165 feet). **3b.** Begin down to the right from the arête in an area of white, decomposed rock. Jam a crack up through a roof (9) and merge left with the regular line.

Irene's Arete, pitch three

4a. Make strenuous moves up and left past a fixed pin (8), then climb beautiful, steep rock along the arête to a black roof (6). Pull right into the middle of the roof, crank up on big jugs, and exit the roof at a two-inch white crystal (8). Continue up into a groove (7) and work slightly left to a belay on a good ledge at the base of a 90-degree dihedral (160 feet). **4b.** Begin just right of the belay and jam a finger crack up to the black roof (8). **4c.** At the roof, it is possible to stay left and climb the arête (7, no pro) to the belay.

5a. Jam and stem up the dihedral (9), hand traverse up and right, then power up a groove (7) to a lower-angle section of the arête. Run the rope all the way to the notch at the next vertical step and belay (165 feet). **5b.** Work around to the left of the dihedral and up to the arête (7). **5c.** From the belay, pull right around the arête and climb a good crack up to the low-angle section (8).

6a. Though there are easier alternatives, the direct finish is well-protected and thoroughly worth doing. From the highest point, stem across the gap to the vertical wall and undercling/lieback up into a dihedral that is followed to the end of roped climbing (10a, 70 feet). A #3.5 Friend or equivalent may be used here. **6b.** Move down the gully about 60 feet to the east and climb a steep fist crack to scrambling terrain (8). **6c.** Descend the gully about 150 feet to the east and make a few steep moves (5) to reach a low-angle slab. From here, scramble northwest to the ridge crest.

Descent. Scramble along the crest of the ridge, first on the right, then on the left to avoid a tower. Once on the slopes of Disappointment Peak, follow a faint path westward through scrub evergreens to the second gully west of IRENE'S ARETE. This is the Southwest Couloir and it is the easiest way to return to the base of the climb and the Caves area. About a third of the way down, the gully is blocked by a large chockstone. Rappel 60 feet from slings, or pass it by scrambling across to the east and downclimbing an easy chimney. Continue down the steep, loose gully, staying mostly to the right but avoid a righthand branch that leads more to the west.

One also may scramble down to the east and pick up the Amphitheater Lake Trail, which connects with the lower switchbacks of the Garnet Canyon Trail. The Grand Teton U.S.G.S. quadrangle (map) will be useful when making this descent for the first time. Work down to the east to a plateau that is above and west-southwest of Amphitheater Lake. Stay to the south of the Spoon Couloir (the long, narrow gully) and descend to the east via ledges and short cliffs until it is possible to curve around north to the lake. Find the trail at the east end of the lake.

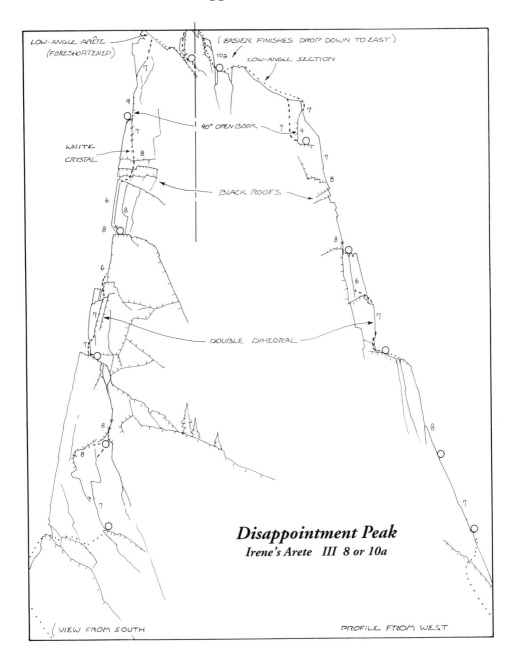

LOW-ANGLE ARÊTE
(FORESHORTENED)

(EASIER FINISHES DROP DOWN TO EAST)

10a

LOW-ANGLE SECTION

7

7

9

7

90° OPEN BOOK

7

9

7

WHITE
CRYSTAL

8

BLACK ROOFS

8

6

8

8

8

6

6

7

7

7

DOUBLE DIHEDRAL

8

7

8

8

8

7

Disappointment Peak
Irene's Arete   III 8 or 10a

(VIEW FROM SOUTH

PROFILE FROM WEST

Middle Teton from the north

Middle Teton

THE MIDDLE TETON (12,804 FT.), the third highest peak in the range, is not exactly a molehill, but in a more remote location it might be less popular. Because it sits squarely at the head of Garnet Canyon, immediately adjacent to the busy south side of the Grand Teton, a certain degree of prestige and notoriety is guaranteed – and it does offer several worthy routes. The SOUTHWEST COULOIR is one of the more popular Teton scrambles, while the MIDDLE TETON GLACIER and NORTHWEST ICE COULOIR provide sweeping ascents on classic alpine terrain. The view from the summit is wholly spectacular and provides an excellent reconnaissance of the south ridges of the Grand Teton. The summit first was reached via the Ellingwood Couloir on August 29, 1923 by Albert Ellingwood, solo.

This brief description of the Middle Teton begins at the Lower Saddle, above which the pinnacled north ridge climbs directly to the summit, passing en route a lesser protuberance called the North Peak. To the east of the ridge is the precipitous north face, with its steep cracks and dihedrals. Below and to the left is the Middle Teton Glacier, which spans the entire northeast face and climbs as a narrow finger of snow and ice to the col between the Dike Pinnacle and main summit. The Dike Pinnacle (about 12,400 ft.) is a subsidiary summit on the east ridge.

The broad east ridge begins just above the Meadows in Garnet Canyon, and culminates in the Dike Pinnacle, beyond which is the east-facing headwall of the summit. A prominent diabase dike splits the east ridge, but veers off to the north of the Dike Pinnacle and traverses the entire north side of the peak. Above the South Fork of Garnet Canyon, the south face forms a complexity of ridges and couloirs, including the Ellingwood Couloir, which reaches the col behind the Dike Pinnacle

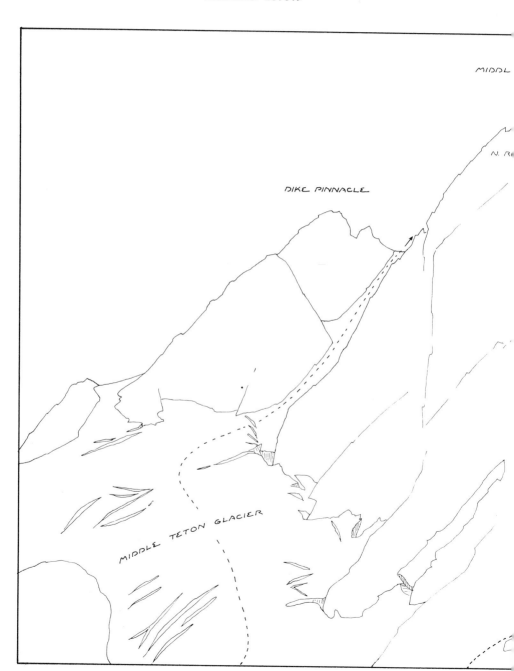

MIDDL

N. R

DIKE PINNACLE

MIDDLE TETON GLACIER

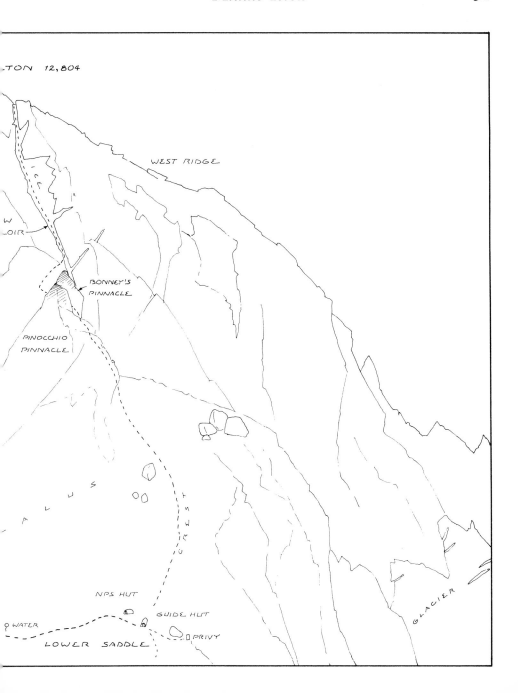

from the southeast. The unnamed saddle between the Middle Teton and South Teton (about 11,300 ft.) sits to the southwest of the summit and overlooks Iceflow Lake below to the west. Above the saddle, the long, low-angle SOUTHWEST COULOIR leads directly to the notch between the north and south summits, the latter of which is slightly lower.

Southwest Couloir
Grade II   moderate snow and rock scramble

THIS IS ONE OF THE MOST popular scrambles in the Tetons. It also is the easiest way to descend from the summit. In early season, the couloir yields a fine, moderate snow climb, but by August, one most likely will find a long, pleasant hike up talus with a bit of scrambling in the steeper, upper section. An ice axe and mountain boots are recommended for the ascent. To reach the bottom of the couloir, take the Garnet Canyon Trail to the Meadows (see Grand Teton), cross the stream, and hike up the South Fork of Garnet Canyon (no distinct trail) all the way to the saddle between the Middle and South Tetons. Hike northeast up the obvious gully to within about 100 feet of the top, move left a bit, and scramble to the north summit. Stretches of snow may be avoided by working up the rock on either side of the couloir. To reach the higher north summit, be sure to finish to the left of the couloir. Allow about 5 hours to reach the summit from the Meadows in Garnet Canyon, and seven or eight hours from Lupine Meadows. This route first was climbed by H. Oswald Christensen, Morris Christensen and Irven Christensen on July 16, 1927.

Northwest Ice Couloir
Grade III   6

THE NORTHWEST COULOIR IS A FIRST-CLASS, if moderate, alpine climb and serves as an excellent primer for its big brothers, such as the BLACK ICE COULOIR on the Grand Teton. In early season, the couloir may be packed with snow, and will present little challenge beyond working up a sweat kicking steps. But later, after the seasonal snow has melted off, a fine ice climb is revealed. This hanging couloir lies to the right of the north ridge and tops out at a notch on the west ridge, very near

The Northwest Couloir lies down and right from the summit

the north summit. It is narrow at the bottom and top and reaches an angle of approximately 50 degrees. Ice screws and a light rock-climbing rack are recommended. Approach via Garnet Canyon and the Lower Saddle (see Grand Teton). To descend from the summit, scramble down the SOUTHWEST COULOIR or downclimb and rappel the north ridge to the notch formed by an eroded dike, then reverse the beginning of the route. The first ascent was made by Peter Lev and James Greig on June 16, 1961.

From the Lower Saddle, scramble up to the base of two small rock towers, Pinocchio Pinnacle (the one furthest north), and Bonney's Pinnacle (the higher of the two). Pass Pinocchio on the west, go through the notch, pass Bonney's on the east, and arrive at a notch formed by an eroded diabase dike. Work up to the left, then back to the right and follow a ledge around into the NORTHWEST COULOIR. A climb of about 700 feet on snow or ice will bring one to a notch on the west ridge, from which an easy scramble leads to the north summit.

Glacier Route
Grade III 4

THIS CLASSIC ROUTE ASCENDS the Middle Teton Glacier to the col behind the Dike Pinnacle, then climbs a steep, narrow couloir up the east-facing summit headwall. In early season, this is one of the few pure glacier and snow climbs in the Tetons. By mid-season, one may expect some moderate rock climbing on the headwall. An ice axe and mountain boots are essential, as well as a minimal rock climbing rack. Snow flukes or pickets may be useful for belays on the steeper sections, and perhaps even ice screws should be carried in late season. This route first was climbed on August 4, 1944 by Sterling Hendricks and Paul Bradt.

Hike the Garnet Canyon Trail to about 10,800 feet, where it is relatively easy to cut south onto the broad apron of the Middle Teton Glacier. Work up and left around the bergschrund, and ascend the steep snow gully directly to the col at the west side of the Dike Pinnacle. Climb a steep, narrow couloir to the notch between the summits or work up slabs and snow patches to the left. The higher north summit is to the right from the notch.

The top of the couloir, Glacier Route

Paul Gagner photo

The Grand Teton

A CITADEL OF NAKED ROCK, steep ice gullies, and hanging snowfields, The Grand Teton towers 7000 feet above the valley of Jackson Hole and is, in both image and elevation, the greatest peak of the range. From a climber's perspective, the broad assortment of excellent routes and the relatively short approach by trail make the Grand Teton an irresistible objective It is, not surprisingly, the most popular of the Teton summits. The climbs range in kind from moderate trade routes such as the OWEN-SPALDING and EXUM RIDGE to the long, complex alpine imperatives of the NORTH RIDGE and the BLACK ICE COULOIR. With such a glorious visage, proximity to civilization, and high concentration of established classic lines, is there another mountain in all the Western Hemisphere to rival the Grand Teton? Most unlikely.

This great peak, from which Grand Teton National Park takes its name, has a rich and complex climbing history, the mere highlights of which are beyond the scope of this presentation. However, the first ascent of the mountain cannot be neglected. Though earlier visits to the summit are claimed by two other parties, the first ascent of the Grand Teton is usually credited to William Owen, Franklin Spalding, Frank Peterson and John Shive, who reached the summit on August 11, 1898. Their route, now known as the OWEN-SPALDING, is the most moderate and popular on the peak and is, with rare exception, the only route used to descend from the summit. An excellent history of early climbing is found in *Mountaineering in the Tetons, the Pioneer Period 1898 to 1940*, by Fritiof Fryxell. More information also is available in *A Complete Climber's Guide to the Teton Range*, by Leigh Ortengburger and Reynold Jackson which, in two volumes, gives historical anecdotes and first ascent information for all known routes in the range.

From the Jenny Lake ranger station, the Grand Teton is completely eclipsed by Teewinot Mountain, but from most other locations in Jackson Hole, its powerful yet graceful summit is wholly apparent and stands as the centerpiece in two unique groupings of peaks. From the plains to the east, it is seen as the northernmost feature of the skyline trinity, Les Trois Teton, along with the Middle and South Tetons. From the northeast, it appears in the Cathedral Group where, framed by Teewinot Mountain and Mount Owen, it rises in breathtaking relief above Cascade Canyon.

Clockwise Description of Peak. The Lower Saddle is the broad col between the Middle Teton and Grand Teton, and is the normal start and/or finish to every outing on the peak. During the summer, one will find here running water, an outdoor toilet, a guide hut, a park ranger hut and several stone enclosures for bivouacs (see map on pages 16-17). To the northwest, a broad gully leads to the Upper Saddle, which is the high col between the main summit (13,770 ft.) and the Enclosure (13,100 ft.). The latter is the massive west buttress of the Grand Teton, which terminates in a minor summit where a mysterious stone enclosure was discovered in 1872 and for which the feature is named.

To the north of the Upper Saddle is the Black Ice Couloir and the remote cirque of Valhalla Canyon. The east wall of this canyon is formed by Mount Owen and a narrow ridge that connects – via a gap called Gunsight Notch – with the north ridge of the Grand Teton. The south side of this ridge, the Grandstand, is a strategic feature in the North Ridge route and its variations. To the east of the ridge is the precipitous alpine cirque of the Teton Glacier, which lies between the north face of the Grand Teton and the south face of Mount Owen. The longest continuous rampart of the peak is the east ridge, which begins just south of the snout of the Teton Glacier (at about 10,200 ft.) and climbs without interruption to the summit. To the southeast, the summit of Disappointment Peak (11,618 ft.) is isolated from the Grand Teton by a narrow col and the gendarme of the Red Sentinel.

The southeast face of the main peak forms the steep, shallow cirque of the Tepee Glacier, the headwall of which holds the uniquely-shaped Otterbody Snowfield. To the left of the glacier is Tepee Pillar, the familiar guardian of the North Fork of Garnet Canyon. The south face of the Grand Teton is formed by three steep ridges, the Underhill, Petzoldt and Exum, from east to west, of which only the latter forms a continuous line to the summit. All three ridges rise from a dike of black diabase that cuts across the entire southern exposure of the peak at the 12,160-foot level, from the notch behind the Red Sentinel, to the shoulder above the Lower Saddle. The Exum Ridge, which might be thought of as the true south ridge of the peak, forms the eastern margin of the broad gully above the Lower Saddle.

Garnet Canyon Trail. By far the most common approach to the Grand Teton is from the east via Garnet Canyon. A fine trail begins from the Lupine Meadows parking area, makes long switchbacks up the forested east slope of Disappointment Peak, contours around into Garnet Canyon, and after seven miles and a 4,800-foot elevation gain, terminates at the Lower Saddle (at about 11,650 feet). The final steep headwall immediately below the saddle may be breached directly on snow in early season or via rocks to the right, where a heavy rope normally is anchored as a hand rail. The Middle Teton sits dead center at the head of Garnet Canyon and divides the canyon's upper reaches into north and south forks. Note that the main trail stays right of the stream at an area called the Meadows (see below) and follows the North Fork of Garnet Canyon to the Lower Saddle. The South Fork does not have a trail beyond the meadows and terminates at the unnamed col between the Middle and South Tetons.

There are specific areas sanctioned by the Park Service for camping in Garnet Canyon. The lowest of these is The Platforms, where the trail first reaches the stream. Several good sites are at the Meadows (about 9,300 ft.), the beautiful, open area of Garnet Canyon located immediately east of the Middle Teton, just before the canyon bifurcates into north and south forks. This is about 4.7 miles from the trailhead and is the lowest of the campsites. At about 5.5 miles, and after a series of short, steep switchbacks, are the Caves or Petzoldt's Caves (about 10,000 ft.), which are actually dugouts under huge boulders. The Moraine Camp area (about 10,800 ft.) begins at about 6.2 miles. Here, one will find a series of stone enclosures or flattened areas along the lateral moraine of the Middle Teton Glacier. The highest and perhaps most strategic campsite is the Lower Saddle (about 11,650 feet.).

Whereas this scenic perch provides an easier shot at the summit, it often is cold and windy – and is seven long, hard miles from the trailhead. Check with the rangers on water, snow conditions, and bear problems when registering for a climb.

Amphitheater and Surprise Lakes Trail. About three miles up the Garnet Canyon Trail, at the last switchback on the east face of Disappointment Peak, a signed trail continues up to the right. After many short switchbacks, the trail reaches Surprise and Amphitheater Lakes. From here, a climber's path leads north to a small pass, from which a rocky ledge with hand cables (broken) allows safe descent into Glacier Gulch. The Teton Glacier lies to the northwest behind the enormous terminal moraine. From here, one has access to routes on the north face and north ridge of the Grand Teton, Mount Owen and Teewinot Mountain.

Valhalla Canyon. The third and only other practical approach to the Grand Teton is from the north out of Cascade Canyon. Take the boat across Jenny Lake (or walk the trail 1.6 miles around the south side) and hike about three miles up the Cascade Canyon Trail to a point just west of the drainage from Valhalla Canyon. The northwest side of the Grand Teton is visible from here. Ford Cascade Creek (a log crossing normally is available) and follow a climber's path up the steep, forested slope to the right of the torrent into Valhalla Canyon. This approach gives access to the NORTH RIDGE and the BLACK ICE COULOIR.

Valhalla Traverse. There is, however, an important alternative for reaching these remote, north-facing routes. The Valhalla Traverse is a long ledge system that, without significant obstruction, traverses the entire west side of the Grand Teton and connects the Lower Saddle with upper Valhalla Canyon. Since the only reasonable descent from the summit returns to the Lower Saddle via the OWEN-SPALDING route, one may, for example, camp at the Lower Saddle, take the Valhalla Traverse, climb the NORTH RIDGE, and return to camp without having to carry bivouac gear over the summit – the only way to fly.

Looking north toward the Grand Teton from the Lower Saddle, find a cairn on a level section of the southwest ridge that is slightly higher than the Saddle. This cairn marks the beginning of the scree ledge that runs across the west face of the Enclosure. To reach the cairn from the Lower Saddle, hike north on the path about halfway to the Black Dike, cut left and descend into a large scree gully. Cross the gully and make an ascending traverse to the level section of the southwest ridge. When free of snow, a faint trail will be found in this area. Follow the ledge system

The Grand Teton from the Lower Saddle in winter

across the west face to the northwest ridge of the Enclosure and continue around to the north side.

After a short descent (about 20 feet), one must choose an upper or lower version of the traverse. The upper route crosses a bowl (usually on snow or ice) and continues at that level around into the Enclosure Couloir. This probably is the most common approach to the BLACK ICE COULOIR. The lower route crosses the bottom of the bowl and follows a ramp down into the second icefield of the BLACK ICE COULOIR (see topo on page 48). This option is used to reach the NORTH RIDGE or the original version of the BLACK ICE COULOIR via the lower and middle of three ramps, respectively, that diagonal up across the lower west face of the Grand Teton.

Owen-Spalding Route
Grade II 4 to 6

THIS VERY POPULAR AND IMPORTANT route has the distinction of being the easiest route on the Grand Teton. It also is the route by which the peak was first climbed. Though it is perhaps less aesthetic than the EXUM RIDGE and other steeper routes, it has the tactical advantages of being swift and direct, and allows an easy escape in bad weather. It is, thus, almost the only route ever used for descent from the summit and the Enclosure. A controversy has existed over the first ascent of this historic route but credit is given to Franklin Spalding, William Owen, Frank Peterson and John Shive, who climbed to the summit on August 11, 1898.

Approach. Begin from Lupine Meadows parking area and follow the Garnet Canyon Trail to the Lower Saddle. For the very athletic, the climb may be done "car to car" in one long day. Most folks, however, will want to make a high camp or bivouac and take two or three days for the ascent.

The long, initial section of the OWEN-SPALDING route is little more than a steep hike. It begins from the Lower Saddle and follows a blunt rib up the middle of a wide gully to the Upper Saddle (about 13,150 feet). Though there are several ways to do this part of the climb, one has become standard and requires some description.

The Route. A distinct footpath leads directly up the crest of the saddle from the low point to the Black Dike. Please use this path and avoid trampling the fragile tundra vegetation. Above the dike, a prominent rib divides the gully between the southwest ridge and the EXUM RIDGE (right). The first steep tower along this rib is called the Needle. Follow a faint path over rocky terrain to the left (west) of the Needle and continue for several hundred feet to where a chimney/gully with a chockstone cuts back to the east, just above this feature. Do not climb the chimney, but continue to the north until it is possible to traverse back to the right (south) and arrive at the top of the chockstone. Work up and right to a bench at the south side of a large, conspicuous boulder. Now crawl through the tunnel formed by the boulder (the Eye of the Needle) and continue north along a ledge past an exposed move to the upper section of the chockstone chimney/-

The Owen-Spalding rappel

gully. This gully is the cut-off point for the UPPER EXUM RIDGE route. If the tunnel is clogged with snow and ice, it is possible to climb over the boulder.

Follow easy ledges and cross scree/snow to an area of black rock. Make a few steep moves up onto the crest of the central rib, and continue just on its right side for a couple of hundred feet, then work back into the main gully and scramble for another 300 feet to the Upper Saddle. Note that from winter to early summer, this entire section of the route above the Lower Saddle may be climbed on snow to the west of the central rib.

Rope up. From the Upper Saddle, work up and left (east, then north) along a large scree ledge to where it narrows on the exposed west face of the peak. Pass beneath the steep Wittich Crack, and after about 12 feet, reach the Belly Roll, a large detached slab that is managed via a hand traverse along its upper edge. A few more feet, and one encounters another obstacle known as the Crawl. Crawl through this narrow space, or better, drop down and hand traverse along the edge, then regain the ledge and continue to a short, overhanging chimney. Climb the chimney (6) or begin with an easier version just around to the left. The two chimneys merge after a very short way. A second short chimney brings one to a rubble-strewn ledge. This section is known as the Double Chimney and can be fairly difficult when icy.

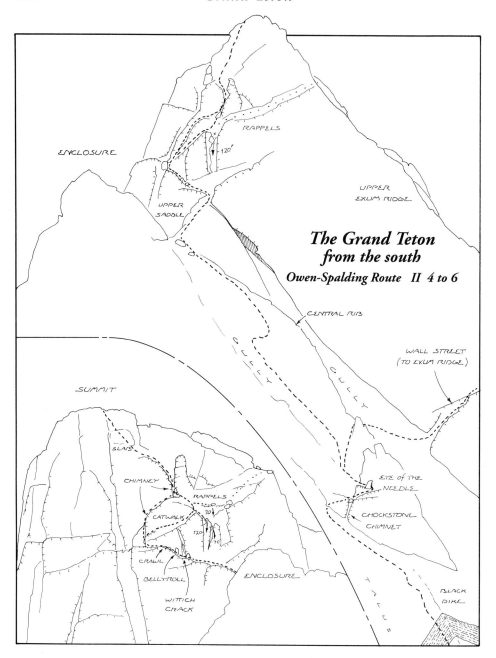

ENCLOSURE

RAPPELS

120'

UPPER SADDLE

UPPER EXUM RIDGE

The Grand Teton from the south

Owen-Spalding Route II 4 to 6

CENTRAL RIB

WALL STREET (TO EXUM RIDGE)

SUMMIT

SLAB

CHIMNEY

RAPPELS

CATWALK

70'

120'

70'

EYE OF THE NEEDLE

CHOCKSTONE CHIMNEY

CRAWL

BELLYROLL

WITTICH CRACK

ENCLOSURE

TALUS

BLACK DIKE

Continue upward via the Owen Chimney (see topo) and traverse southeast to the base of yet another chimney that cuts east-northeast through the upper cliffband. As an easier option, avoid the Owen Chimney and move up and right to gain the Catwalk, a long, sloping ramp that leads south to an overlook above the main rappel. This rappel is commonly used on the descent, and it is a good idea to verify its location at this time. Look for slings around a spike of rock a short way down to the south. From the south end of the Catwalk, scramble northeast up to the chimney in the upper cliffband. Climb the chimney for about 50 feet, then branch off to the left in a dihedral. From the dihedral, an easy though slightly indirect scramble leads northeast to the summit.

The Wittich Crack (6) sometimes is less icy than the regular Double Chimney and adds two pitches of excellent rock to the ascent. Begin at the obvious vertical crack system about 12 feet before reaching the Belly Roll (see topo), climb straight up, and belay in an alcove beneath an overhang. Climb out around the left side of the overhang and arrive midway along the Catwalk. This was first climbed by Hans Wittich, Walter Becker and Rudolph Weidner on June 27, 1931.

Descent. It is very important to pay close attention to the direction of travel and notable features of the ascent as one proceeds, since the route – at least to the rappel – must be reversed to get back to the Upper Saddle. The value of this will be particularly evident in the event of bad weather. From the summit, downclimb about 300 feet to the southwest to reach the top of the dihedral and chimney in the upper cliffband. After descending the chimney, continue another 100 feet to the southwest past the Catwalk to the top of the main rappel. Look for slings around a six-foot block about 40 feet to the south of the Catwalk. Rappel 120 feet to reach the scree ledge, then scramble down to the Upper Saddle. In the event one has only a single, standard length rope, there is an alternate rappel route that begins on a ledge up to the southeast of the main rappel. From slings around a block, rappel 70 feet to a chockstone in a chimney. Make a second 70-foot rappel to reach the scree ledge just south of the main rappel finish. It also is reasonable, in dry conditions, to downclimb the entire OWEN-SPALDING route from the summit to the Upper Saddle.

The easiest line of descent from the Upper Saddle is to reverse the standard route and go back through the Eye of the Needle. Remember to head southwest at first to avoid the more difficult gully between the central rib and the Exum Ridge. After 300 feet, descend from the crest of the rib for 200 feet and drop back west into the main gully at the area of black rock. Continue down past the Exum Ridge cut-off and pass through the Eye of the Needle (see above). Traverse back northwest into the chockstone chimney and climb down to the chockstone, then continue northwest across a slab to get back into the main gully. This is all fairly obvious on location. Scramble down a bit southeast to the Black Dike, pick up the footpath on the crest of the tundra ridge, and follow it down to the Lower Saddle.

Exum Ridge

THE OWEN-SPALDING AND THE EXUM RIDGE are the two most popular routes on the Grand Teton. Whereas the OWEN-SPALDING is the easiest line on the summit, being no more than a steep hike for most of its course, the EXUM RIDGE is more of a climbing challenge. Solid rock, interesting route-finding, and a commanding position along the south ridge of the highest peak in the range, combine to yield one of the classic ascents of North America. Most parties climb only the upper, more moderate section of the ridge by traversing in along a ledge known as Wall Street. The lower section is considerably steeper and more difficult, but if skill and experience allow, the entire 2500-foot ascent from the black dike is highly recommended.

The Exum or South Ridge is easily identified from the Lower Saddle as the serrated skyline ridge which descends from the summit and forms the right (east) margin of the broad gully above and north of the Lower Saddle. The upper section was first climbed by Glenn Exum, who soloed the route as the maiden voyage of his climbing career on July 15, 1931. The entire ridge, beginning from the black dike, was first climbed by Jack Durrance and Ken Henderson on September 1, 1936.

The route is described here in sequence, beginning at the black dike. The ascent of the entire South Ridge usually is referred to as the COMPLETE or DIRECT EXUM RIDGE. To descend from the summit, it is possible to reverse the route to Wall Street, but it is much easier to downclimb the OWEN-SPALDING route (see above) and make the 120-foot rappel to the Upper Saddle, then scramble down the gully via the Eye of the Needle to the Lower Saddle.

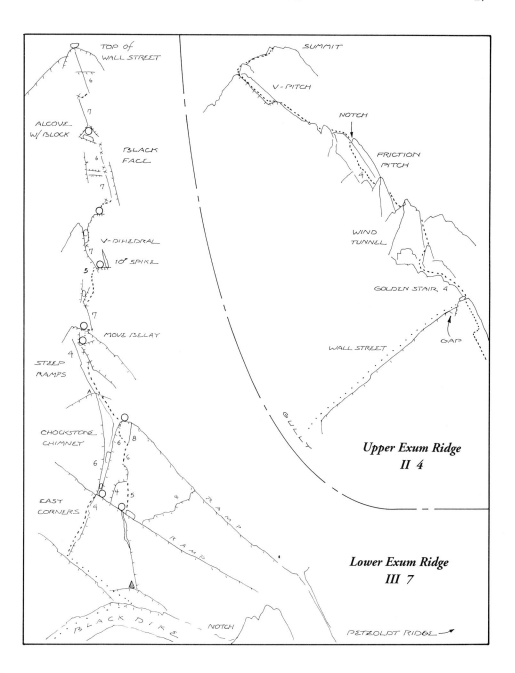

TOP of
WALL STREET

6

7

ALCOVE
W/ BLOCK

BLACK
FACE

6

7

V-DIHEDRAL

7

10' SPIKE

5

7

MOVE BELAY

4

STEEP
RAMPS

A

CHOCKSTONE
CHIMNEY

6   8

6

6   6

EAST
CORNERS   4

4   5

4

RAMP

RAMP

BLACK DIKE   NOTCH

SUMMIT

V-PITCH

NOTCH

FRICTION
PITCH

4

WIND
TUNNEL

GOLDEN STAIR 4

GAP

WALL STREET

GULLY

**Upper Exum Ridge
II 4**

**Lower Exum Ridge
III 7**

PETZOLDT RIDGE

Lower Exum Ridge
Grade III 7

FROM THE LOWER SADDLE, follow the path northward through the tundra as for the OWEN-SPALDING route. At a point short of the dike, break off to the right (east) and follow a faint path up over a promontory and contour along to a ledge directly beneath the large chimney of the first pitch. This chimney appears, from the Lower Saddle, as a large, west-facing dihedral. Most parties will want to rope up here. An easy initial pitch works around to the left, up corners, and through a bulge (4) to reach the ledge beneath the chimney. A more difficult start ascends a steep, left-facing dihedral that begins at a cairn on the next ledge up. However, the easiest way to reach the chimney is to continue further along the black dike toward the Petzolt Ridge and follow a long, grassy ramp back left to the ledge.

1a. Climb the large chimney past two chockstones (6) to reach a pedestal at the top of another long ramp (135 feet). **1b.** Climb the south-facing wall to the right of the chimney and work back left near the top (6). The cracks that continue straight up are more difficult (8 or 9).

2. Follow an easy ramp up to the left, then climb a dihedral and crack to a belay alcove just below a major step in the ridge (6, 150 feet). Move the belay up to the next steep section.

3. Jam up a hand crack to a wedged block, then work up and right to belay on a sandy ledge with a 10-foot detached flake (7; 100 feet).

4. Grunt up a flared chimney with a wide crack (7) to a tunnel, up around either side of a chockstone (6), and up a short crack to a small ledge at the base of the Black Face (65 feet).

5. If only the whole climb were like the next two pitches! Above rises a near-vertical face of exquisite black and gold rock that yields the hardest climbing on the route, yet never lacks for good holds. Move up and right past a fixed pin, up a steep crack just left of a right-facing dihedral, then up past a series of fixed pins to an alcove above a detached block (7; 110 feet).

6. Jam straight up a flared hand crack to a fixed pin, traverse right, and ascend another crack to the top of Wall Street (7; 110 feet). It is possible – but not recommended – to avoid this pitch by working around to the left on easier terrain.

The Black Face, Lower Exum Ridge

Ted Karasote photo

At this point, it is possible to cross the gap to the west via hand traverse or short rappel and scramble off on Wall Street, or continue to the summit via the original Exum Ridge route along the crest of the upper south ridge.

Upper Exum Ridge
Grade II   4

TO DO ONLY THIS UPPER SECTION of the ridge, follow the OWEN-SPALDING route to the gully just beyond the Eye of the Needle (see topo on page 40), then scramble east to the crest of the central rib, or better, reach the crest at a gap a short way further north. From here, Wall Street is seen clearly as a long, flat ledge that angles up and right to the skyline of the Exum Ridge. Make a descending traverse into the scree gully to the east and scramble up a smaller side gully to get onto Wall Street. Walk up the broad, flat ledge to where it ends short of the ridge crest. Most parties will want to rope up here.

Cross the gap most easily via hand traverse and belay on a big ledge with a commanding view. You now are on the south ridge of the Grand Teton about 1500 feet from the summit. Climb directly up the crest on solid, knobby rock (4) or work around to the northeast and ascend easy cracks back to the crest. The initial step is called the Golden Stair. After about 300 feet, one arrives at a large tower that has miraculously escaped being named. Traverse right (east) for a rope length, then head up either side of a steep gully/chimney system (sometimes icy) called the Wind Tunnel for two pitches. Now head up through terraces and a short chimney on the west side of the crest to reach a ledge at the base of a smooth, clean slab. One also may reach this point via a crack on the right side of the crest.

The next rope length is known as the Friction Pitch because people get into arguments about who has to lead it. No, seriously, this is the crux of the upper ridge; it is smooth and rather poorly protected. Move up and slightly left on friction to two knobs, up and right to a shallow groove, then upward to the top of the slab. Now scramble up and right to a small notch that may contain snow or ice. Work northwest along the right side of the ridge for some 300 feet until it is possible to move left into a prominent, left-facing dihedral/ramp called the V-Pitch, or Open Book. Pass the dihedral in 150 feet, then scramble across an easy section to the next step in the ridge. Move down a bit to the west and make an awkward lieback to pass this step. Note that from the base of the step, it is possible to make a descending northwest traverse to the top of the OWEN-SPALDING rappel as a means of escape.

Continue up to another step, which is passed via a short crack and follow the ridge crest to the base of the summit block. Traverse east about 50 feet, then angle up over broken ground to the summit. There also is a good alternate finish called the Horse. From the base of the summit block, traverse around to its west side and climb up to a knife-edged ridge (the Horse, of course), and follow it to the summit.

The Black Ice Couloir
Grade IV 6

The BLACK ICE COULOIR is, rightly, thought of as *the* alpine ice climb of the Tetons. It was the first major route of its kind to be done in the range and now stands among the great classic climbs of North America. After at least two earlier attempts, it was first climbed by Raymond Jacquot and Herb Swedlund on July 29, 1961. It was the first route to reach the Upper Saddle from the north and is the most sought-out Teton ice climb.

The ascent is long and involved, hidden in the depths of the remote north-facing cleft between the west face of the Grand Teton and north buttress of the Enclosure. There are three distinct icefields, each separated by sections of rock, and a final, narrow chute that leads to the Upper Saddle. The route is difficult to reach by any approach, escape is almost impossible, and it is steep, cold, shadowed, and subject to rockfall. The very name reeks of drama and invokes a certain sense of awe and anxiety. Not for the novitiate, this challenging route requires developed skills in route finding, the use of pitons and ice screws, and the ability to move quickly over mixed terrain with full alpine gear. Bring crampons, six to eight ice screws, a light rock-climbing rack, and a few pitons up to one-half inch. The route may be done without pitons but good nut placements are scarce.

Approach. There are several logistical options for this ascent that depend upon path of approach and whether one plans a retrievable high camp, a carry-over, or a one-day marathon ascent. The most direct approach with the least hiking is via Valhalla Canyon (see topo). The BLACK ICE COULOIR begins from the head of this canyon and climbs for about 2200 feet to the Upper Saddle. If camp is made in the canyon,

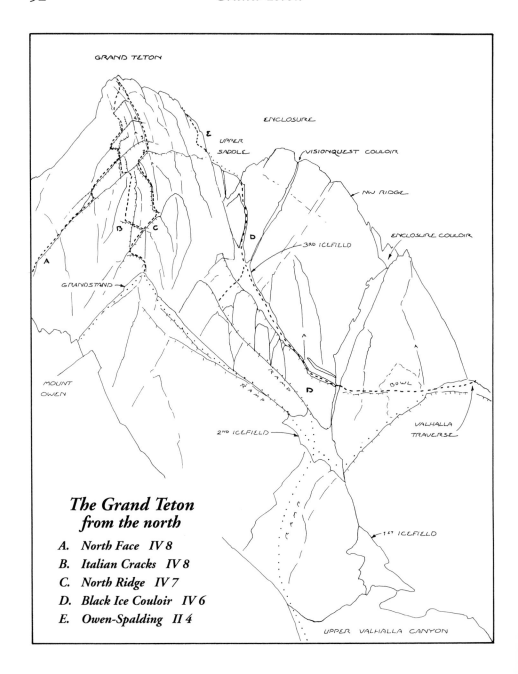

**The Grand Teton
from the north**

A. *North Face   IV 8*
B. *Italian Cracks   IV 8*
C. *North Ridge   IV 7*
D. *Black Ice Couloir   IV 6*
E. *Owen-Spalding   II 4*

The Grand Teton from the northwest

all overnight gear must be carried up the route; thus, a one-day blitz might be preferable with this approach. Since the only reasonable descent is via the OWEN-SPALDING route, it is, however, possible to retrieve a camp in Valhalla Canyon by taking the Valhalla Traverse (see above) back to the north from the Lower Saddle.

The most popular two-day alternative is to hike the Garnet Canyon Trail and camp at the Lower Saddle. From there, the Valhalla Traverse is followed around into the BLACK ICE COULOIR. Descent via the OWEN-SPALDING route brings one directly back to camp.

The Route from the Lower Saddle. Start early and follow the Valhalla Traverse around the west side of the Grand Teton to the northwest ridge of the Enclosure. Do not descend into Valhalla Canyon but contour around to the east on a ramp that leads to a small basin or bowl. Cross the upper part of the bowl – which may contain snow or ice – and follow a marginal ledge system around a buttress, back into the Enclosure Couloir. Cross the couloir and ascend the lower of two diagonal

Topping out above the crux, Black Ice Couloir

Paul Gagner photo

ramps. This ramp traverses the north buttress of the Enclosure and leads directly into the third icefield of the BLACK ICE COULOIR. Above the icefield, the couloir closes into a steep, narrow chute. One reaches the 70-degree crux about 120 feet up into the chute, beyond which a partially protected belay niche will be found on the right. One last (easier) pitch leads to the Upper Saddle. There are seven or eight pitches of ice from the bottom of the third icefield; some of these may be snow-covered in early season. Be alert for rockfall. The safest and most direct line is to follow the west margin of the ice and belay from pitons or ice screws along the north buttress of the Enclosure.

The Route from Valhalla Canyon. From the upper slopes of Valhalla Canyon, it is possible to climb directly up into the BLACK ICE COULOIR by ascending the first two icefields, angling right into the Enclosure Couloir, then proceeding as described above. While this has the appeal of having "done the whole thing," it also exposes the climber to the maximum hazard from rockfall. The wiser choice probably is to follow the line of the first ascent which, while bypassing the lower third of the main couloir, makes for an excellent alpine ascent.

The Original Route. Before reaching the very bottom of the BLACK ICE COULOIR, work up and left and gain a ramp that leads directly into the second of the three obvious icefields. To the right is the bottom of the Enclosure Couloir, ahead and to the left (east), three large ramps angle up and left onto the west face of the Grand Teton. Ascend the middle ramp - which sometimes begins with a narrow runnel of ice - for about 500 feet to an area of black rock. Work up and right on broken rock and snow ledges for one or two pitches and arrive at the broad, central (third) icefield of the BLACK ICE COULOIR. Note that the third icefield occupies the third (upper) diagonal ramp. Climb up and across the icefield to the southwest and enter the narrow and final section of the climb.

North Ridge
Grade IV 7

If the ascent of any one route could qualify as the penultimate Teton experience, it might be the NORTH RIDGE of the Grand Teton. Probably the most difficult route in North America at the time of its first ascent, it has withstood the test of time and still is considered a serious undertaking by experienced alpinists. The NORTH RIDGE was first climbed on July 19, 1931 by Robert Underhill and Fritiof Fryxell.

The route begins atop the Grandstand, the massive north shoulder of the Grand Teton that connects with Mount Owen at Gunsight Notch and forms the headwall of the Teton Glacier. Above the Grandstand, the route ascends a series of ramps and chimneys and finishes on the northwest arête. One may also finish with the last few pitches of the NORTH FACE route, which adds notably to the overall difficulty of the ascent. The NORTH RIDGE is a true alpine climb and typically will require use of an ice axe, crampons, and mountain boots in addition to full rock climbing gear. Under rare, late season conditions, the entire route from Valhalla Canyon will be dry and free of snow and ice, but for the small ice patch at the base of the Chockstone Chimney. It is possible, however, to climb up and around the ice on the left (9).

Approach. The Grandstand, from which the route proceeds, may be approached from the east via the Teton Glacier or from the west via Valhalla Canyon; the latter has become more popular. To utilize the eastern option, begin from Lupine Meadows, hike the Garnet Canyon Trail for several miles, and take the cutoff to Amphitheater Lake. From the lake, follow a climber's path north into Glacier Gulch,

**The Grand Teton
from the north**

A.   **North Face   IV 8**
B.   **Italian Cracks   IV 8**
C.   **North Ridge   IV 7**
D.   **Black Ice Couloir   IV 6**
E.   **Owen-Spalding   II 4**

scramble up over the terminal moraine, work up the steepening Teton Glacier, and cross the moat (the gap between the glacier and the rock) to the Grandstand. The easiest line on the east face of the Grandstand is typically along its left margin and it is no piece of cake. One can expect rockfall from the north face and tricky route finding on steep snow and wet slabs. Just crossing the moat can be an ordeal.

To reach the top of the Grandstand from the west, one has the same options as for the BLACK ICE COULOIR. Currently, the most popular and practical version is to make a very early start from the Lower Saddle and take the Valhalla Traverse (see above) around the west side of the Grand Teton to where it crosses the northwest ridge of the Enclosure. Drop down into Valhalla Canyon at the level of the second icefield of the BLACK ICE COULOIR and make an ascending traverse onto the lower of three large ramps that diagonals up across the west face to the top of the Grandstand. One may expect wet slabs, snow, ice, or all of the above along this ramp, but much of this can be avoided in late season by staying as far left as possible. The ramp is a scramble in dry conditions.

The Route. From the top of the Grandstand, scramble up beside a large block and belay.

1. Go left behind the block, then up and left (6) to a ledge that is followed east to a gully. Scramble up the gully and belay on a bench.
2. Continue up steeper terrain to a usually snow-covered shelf at the base of the notorious Chockstone Chimney (4). An ice axe is normally needed at this point to cut steps up into the chimney.
3. Climb directly up the steep chimney, pass the chockstone on the left (7 to 9 depending on who tells the story), and belay just above.
4. Continue up the chimney and belay at its top (6). This and the previous pitch may be done as one.
5. Climb a steep slab with poor protection, first going up and left to the arête (6 to 7), then back to the right, to arrive at the Second Ledge of the NORTH FACE route (see topo). This pitch is very difficult if iced up, and may require crampons.
6. Traverse up and right along the ledge to the west side of the ridge, which at this point could be described as the northwest arête. Climb up to the Third Ledge of the NORTH FACE route and belay.
7. Follow a left-facing corner and chimney system to the Fourth Ledge and belay (7).

8. Continue in the same system for another pitch (7) beyond which 400 feet of scrambling lead to the summit.

For a more rapid ascent from the Second Ledge (top of pitch five) it is possible to traverse right, almost to the Great West Chimney, and scramble to the summit. To escape the route from the Second Ledge, continue all the way across the west face to the Crawl of the OWEN-SPALDING route, whence one may descend to the Lower Saddle.

The Italian Cracks Variation
Grade IV 7 or 8

THIS IS A HIGH-QUALITY ALTERNATIVE to the difficult chimney and slab pitches of the regular NORTH RIDGE route. It was first climbed by Howard Friedman and Peter Woolen on August 19, 1971. The line follows a fairly direct series of cracks out on the north face, around to the left of the immense dihedral of the Chockstone Chimney. Begin the variation about 15 feet from the east end of the long ledge at the top of the regular first pitch.

2. Climb a wide crack for about 20 feet, then traverse 15 feet left into an easier system (6). Turn a small roof after about 120 feet and belay on a ledge (7; 150 feet). It also is possible to climb straight up from the ledge (8) and merge left nearer to the roof.
3. Work up and around the left side of a roof and belay after 120 feet (7).
4. Moderate face climbing leads to the Second Ledge (5; 75 feet).

North Face Finish
Grade IV 8

THIS VARIATION WAS FIRST COMPLETED FROM the regular NORTH RIDGE route by Jim Donini, Rick Black and Michael Cole on August 11, 1976. The option adds three pitches of steep climbing to the regular route or to the Italian Cracks. Looking east down the Second Ledge from the regular route, locate a black chimney between two right-facing dihedrals.

5. Climb the black chimney (7) to the Third Ledge of the NORTH FACE route (see below) and belay.
6. Move the belay about 20 feet down to the east to the bottom of a right-facing

Second Ledge, North Face Route   Paul Gagner photo

dihedral. This is the Pendulum Pitch. Ascend the dihedral for about half a rope (6), traverse left and around a corner on a sloping ledge (8), and go up to a recess at the east end of the Fourth Ledge.

7. Move the belay 100 feet or more westward up the Fourth Ledge. Traverse back left (east) to a small, right-facing dihedral and climb to its top. Then, traverse up and left on friction (7) for about 35 feet to reach the "V," a large recess in the upper north face from which a scramble of several hundred feet brings one to the summit.

North Face
Grade IV 8

NO COLLECTION OF TETON CLASSICS would be complete without the NORTH FACE of the Grand Teton. Steeped in shadow on the cold side of the mountain, this complex, mixed route is one of the great alpine challenges of the range. The face first was climbed on August 25, 1936 by Paul and Eldon Petzoldt; though they finished the route via the upper NORTH RIDGE, the ascent was made from Jenny Lake in a single day. The DIRECT NORTH FACE, which now is the standard line, ascends the very steep upper wall to the left of the NORTH RIDGE, and was pieced together by different parties between 1941 and 1953. The entire route, including the first free ascent of the Pendulum Pitch and the final traverse into the "V," was completed by Richard Emerson, Willi Unsoeld and Leigh Ortenburger on July 24, 1953. The face, which is about 2500 feet high, tends to hold snow and ice on ledges, and has considerable hazard from rockfall on the initial pitches. Due to the great height of the face, speed of ascent is of the essence. An ice axe and crampons will be useful, as well as full rock climbing gear up to three inches.

Approach via the Teton Glacier as described for the NORTH RIDGE (see above). Descend from the summit via the OWEN-SPALDING route.

The Route. From the upper part of the Teton Glacier, note that there are two large chimneys to the left of the bottom of the Grandstand. Cross the moat and move up and left onto a ledge system at the base of the left chimney. The right (more westerly) chimney is loose and dangerous and should not be climbed. It also is possible to avoid most of the glacier and the moat by ascending a long, diagonal ledge up to the base of the left chimney. Ascend the chimney for several moderate pitches, then move up and right along a ledge system to Guano Chimney (6), a

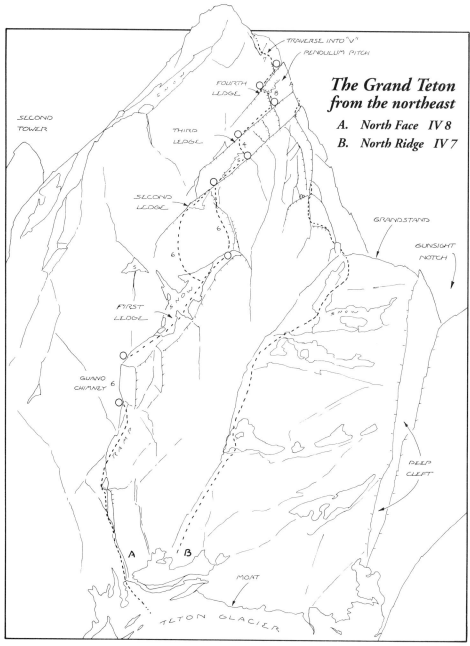

TRAVERSE INTO "V"

PENDULUM PITCH

FOURTH LEDGE

SECOND TOWER

THIRD LEDGE

The Grand Teton from the northeast

A. North Face IV 8
B. North Ridge IV 7

SECOND LEDGE

GRANDSTAND

GUNSIGHT NOTCH

FIRST LEDGE

GUANO CHIMNEY

SNOW

DEEP CLEFT

A   B

MOAT

TETON GLACIER

deep cleft that leads to the First Ledge (see topo). About 100 feet up the First Ledge, above the chimney, is a cave that can be used for a bivouac.

Scramble all the way to the west end of the First Ledge. Climb a steep, shallow chimney for about 130 feet (6) and belay, then work up and left on easy friction to reach the Second Ledge. Scramble up to the right for three or four hundred feet until an obvious break leads directly up to the Third Ledge. Scramble another 400 hundred feet or so up the Third Ledge to a right-facing dihedral just short of a bunch of rappel slings. This is the start to the Pendulum Pitch – it is also a good place to exit the face in the event of nightfall or foul weather. To escape, rappel 120 feet to the Second Ledge, traverse up and westward to intersect the north ridge, then traverse the west face to the Upper Saddle.

Ascend the dihedral for about half a rope (7), work left on a sloping, tapering ledge, make a blind traverse left (8), and crank up into a black alcove at the east end of the Fourth Ledge. Move the belay about 100 feet up the ledge to start the last, difficult pitch. This is only about 50 feet from the north ridge. Traverse back left (east) to a small, right-facing dihedral and climb to its top. Now, traverse up and left on friction (7) for about 35 feet to reach the "V," a large recess in the upper north face from which a scramble of several hundred feet leads to the summit.

Mount Owen

MOUNT OWEN, THE SECOND HIGHEST of the Teton summits, is the centerpiece of a triumvirate that, with Teewinot to the east and the Grand Teton to the south, forms the precipitous cirque of the Teton Glacier. This graceful diadem of jagged ridges and terraced snowfields was the last of the great Teton peaks to be climbed, and its first ascent by Kenneth Henderson, Robert Underhill, Phil Smith, and Fritiof Fryxell, on July 16, 1930, created one of the finest alpine routes in the range.

The East Ridge
Grade II   6

THIS AESTHETIC AND SATISFYING route ascends the terraced snowfields and summit knob from the notch west of the East Prong. It is a true alpine classic requiring an ice axe, mountain boots and rock climbing gear. The ascent develops tremendous relief and scenic grandeur as one moves up the final snowfield toward the knob. A seeming stone's throw to the south, the north face of the Grand Teton looms larger than life, while to the north, Cascade Creek and the southwest ridge of Storm Point appear in miniature 5,500 feet below. Rack up to a #3 Friend or equivalent. Check with the rangers on the advisability of bringing crampons.

Approach. Begin at the Lupine Meadow parking area and hike the Garnet Canyon Trail to the junction for Surprise and Amphitheater Lakes. Follow the right branch of the trail to Amphitheater Lake, which is the traditional campsite for the ascent. Pick up a climber's path and follow it northward through a notch in the northeast ridge of Disappointment Peak, where Mount Owen comes into full view. From here, the east ridge forms the righthand skyline. The prominent gendarme to the east of the upper snowfield is the East Prong. Follow the path down into Glacier Gulch, then make an ascending traverse across the terminal moraine of the Teton Glacier and head for the Koven Couloir, the gully that descends from the notch at the west side of the East Prong.

Descent. It is relatively easy to rappel down the EAST RIDGE and the Koven Couloir. A series of sling anchors exist for this purpose. Two ropes are required. One also may downclimb the KOVEN ROUTE, beginning from the west side of the summit knob (see below).

The Route. From the lower Teton Glacier, work up into the initial section of the Koven Couloir and kick steps (or scramble in late season) up to a small waterfall. Pass this feature on the left and attain a broad, usually snow-covered bench. Above the bench, climb the steep upper couloir to the col (notch) west of the East Prong. This may be done by climbing directly up steep snow or via steep, ledgy terrain on the left side of the couloir. From the notch, head straight west to the next obstacle – a 120-foot rockband. There are several options of ascent at this point, the easiest of which is to traverse about 50 feet north from the crest of the ridge and climb a deep chimney to the upper snowfield. The chockstone near the top of the chimney may be passed on either side.

From here, the climb becomes more dramatic. Ascend the crest of the snowfield to the base of the upper east ridge, where several options exist for passing the steep initial buttress: (a) Perhaps the easiest is to continue on snow for several hundred feet along the north side of the ridge until it is obvious to work up and left along ramps and ledges to gain the lower-angle crest of the ridge. (b) A more difficult and aesthetic option is to climb directly up the northeast arête of the buttress via a 60-foot left-facing dihedral (7) that leads to a belay at a fixed pin. From the pin traverse right about 20 feet and scramble a full rope-length up a shallow gully that leads to the ridge crest. (c) A third option is to climb a moderate chimney system on the south side of the ridge (see topo).

Once on the crest of the ridge, proceed westward up easy slabs for a couple of hundred feet to a ledge with slings. Climb a moderate gully on the south side of the crest for a full rope-length to an alcove at the base of the summit knob. The final

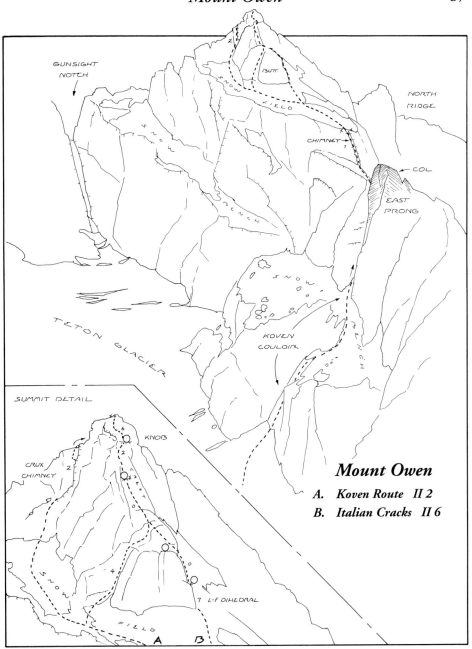

GUNSIGHT
NOTCH

NORTH
RIDGE

SNOW
FIELD

BUTT.

CHIMNEY

COL

EAST
PRONG

TRENCH

TETON GLACIER

SNOW

KOVEN
COULOIR

TRENCH

SUMMIT DETAIL

6

KNOB

CRUX
CHIMNEY

2

2

CREST

7 L-F DIHEDRAL

SNOW FIELD

A B

Mount Owen

A. Koven Route   II 2
B. Italian Cracks   II 6

event is a steep, 60-foot slab. Begin this last pitch to the right, work up and left to a small flake (6), traverse left on a down-sloping ledge, then shoot straight for the top. The last 30 feet are easier. Three 3⁄8-inch stoppers can be used for protection at strategic points on this pitch.

Koven Route
Grade II 2

ON JULY 20, 1931, THEODORE AND GUSTAV Koven, Paul Petzoldt and Glen Exum reached the summit by a variation of the original EAST RIDGE route and discovered the easiest, and now most popular, route up Mount Owen. In early season, this is an exhilarating snow climb with a short stretch of rock at the top.

Begin as for the EAST RIDGE route, and follow it all the way to the upper snowfield. Instead of climbing up to the base of the rock buttress, traverse left along the shelf – below the apron of snow, if possible – all the way to steep slabs and ledges near the southwest ridge. Head northwest up a long gully to a steep corner. Ascend a 40-foot chimney in the right wall (crux), then move left up steep slabs to reach the crest of the southwest ridge. Follow an easy ledge system north to an area of black rock. Now, work up and right (south) to the base of the deep, west chimney, which is followed for about 40 feet to the summit.

Koven snowfields, Mount Owen   Paul Gagner photo

Teewinot Mountain

TEEWINOT IS ONE OF THE MOST beautiful and compelling peaks in the Teton Range. It is the only alpine peak wholly visible from the main visitor area at Jenny Lake, and with its serrated skyline ridge and shining snow couloirs, it completely dominates the scene. Its prominent position along the eastern slope of the range, directly above the Lupine Meadows parking area, also makes Teewinot the most accessible of the major Teton summits.

East Face

II moderate snow and rock scramble

THE EAST FACE OF TEEWINOT is characterized by a broad couloir that leads directly up to a notch at the south side of the summit. Here lies one of the most compact and enjoyable alpine outings in the Tetons. What it lacks in technical challenge is more than offset by the brevity of the approach, the direct line, the extraordinary setting and the peerless summit view of Mount Owen and the Grand Teton. In early season, the route is a sweeping snow climb requiring an ice axe and mountain boots, but by mid-August, the 5,600-foot ascent may be entirely on rock. Typically, the climb takes 5 to 6 hours from car to summit. The first known ascent was made by Fritiof Fryxell and Phil D. Smith on August 14, 1929.

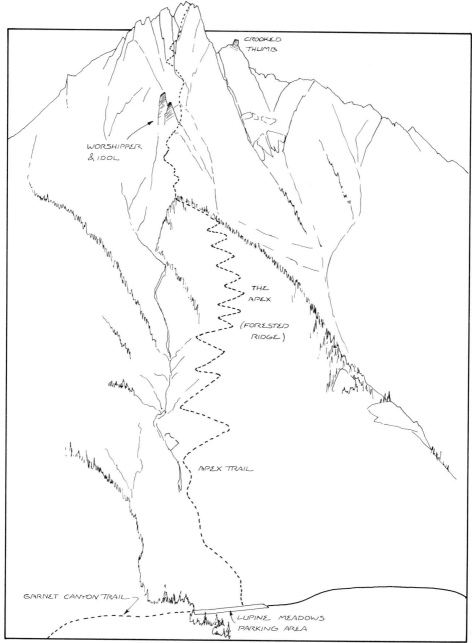

CROOKED
THUMB

WORSHIPPER
& IDOL

THE
APEX

(FORESTED
RIDGE)

APEX TRAIL

GARNET CANYON TRAIL

LUPINE MEADOWS
PARKING AREA

The Apex Trail, which serves as approach to Teewinot, begins along the west side of the Lupine Meadows parking area, about 150 feet from its north end. Follow this trail westward, first through a tangle of scrub vegetation, then up the forested, triangular shoulder (the Apex) below the upper east face of the peak. After a seeming interminable number of switchbacks, one reaches the top of the Apex. The trail continues westward along a wooded ridge, then climbs steeply to a talus field just beneath two prominent gendarmes known as the Worshipper and the Idol (higher). Angle up and right into the broad couloir, where one is likely to begin ascending on snow. In late season, a vaguely discernable path may be followed – with a bit of scrambling – all the way to the summit. The final stretch of the couloir is rather narrow and holds a finger of perennial snow. About 300 feet below the notch, move right and work up easy terrain (or snow) to the right side of the summit area. A short scramble to the west brings one to the tiny exposed summit and into the very heart of the Tetons.

The Worshipper

To descend, reverse the route. A rope may be carried as a safety precaution, but is not ordinarily needed.

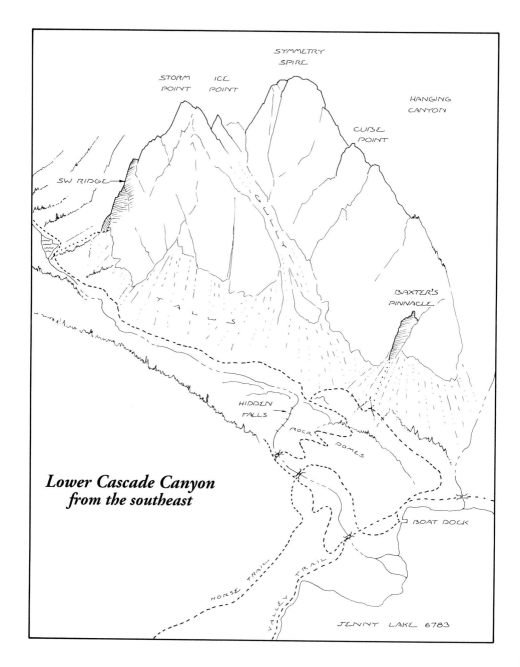

SYMMETRY
SPIRE

STORM
POINT

ICE
POINT

HANGING
CANYON

CUBE
POINT

SW RIDGE

GULLY

BAXTER'S
PINNACLE

FALLS

HIDDEN
FALLS

ROCK

DOMES

**Lower Cascade Canyon
from the southeast**

BOAT DOCK

HORSE TRAIL

VALLEY TRAIL

JENNY LAKE 6783

Storm Point

LOOKING TO THE NORTHWEST from the ranger station at Jenny Lake, a compelling group of crags thrusts up to form a jagged skyline. The highest of these, characterized by a double south buttress, is Symmetry Spire. The southernmost summit, the walls of which drop steeply into Cascade Canyon, is Storm Point. Ice Point lies between. In the Tetons, where the approaches are sometimes more arduous than the routes to which they lead, any decent hunk of rock that can be reached within an hour's walk or so is going to be popular. The route known as GUIDES WALL, on the southwest ridge of Storm Point, has not only a short approach, but beautiful rock, commanding scenery, and an easy descent via rappel. What is more, half of the hike can be foregone by taking the tour boat across Jenny Lake. GUIDES WALL originally was climbed by Richard Pownall and Art Gilkey during the summer of 1949; the more difficult variations were developed over the years by different parties.

Guides Wall
Grade III 7 to 10c

Approach. From the Jenny Lake ranger station, walk south a short way to the boat concession. A boat departs about every thirty minutes (or less) and requires about 10 minutes to reach the mouth of Cascade Canyon. A round trip ticket costs a few dollars. Note that the last launch of the day returns at six in the evening. If travel by boat is ruled out, walk across the bridge at the boat dock and follow the trail 1.6 miles around the south side of Jenny Lake. From the trail junction along the west shore of the lake, hike about 1.8 miles up Cascade Canyon to where a rock slide has caused the formation of a large pond. Turn to face north and you should be looking

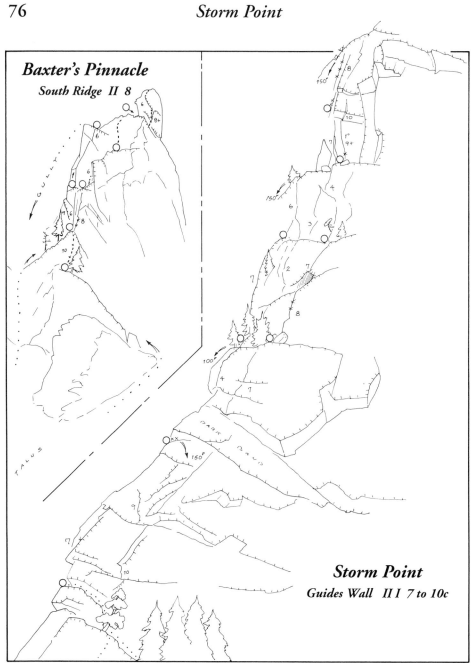

Baxter's Pinnacle
South Ridge II 8

Storm Point
Guides Wall   II I 7 to 10c

directly up the southwest ridge of Storm Point. Hike straight up the rock slide to the first cliffband, scramble right across a convenient ledge, follow a steep path up and right, then move up to the west to the top of the obvious ramp. Rope up.

The Route. From the top of the ramp, scramble behind a tree, go up a steeper ramp to a ledge on the west side of the arête, and set the belay.

1a. Climb a right-facing dihedral with a fixed pin (7) and follow cracks and corners to a two-bolt anchor 15 feet above an obvious ledge (120 feet). **1b.** From behind the initial tree, climb the obvious roof (10a) and the clean dihedrals above to the two-bolt anchor.

2. Climb an undistinguished pitch with harder variations to the right (7) and belay on a broad ledge with two trees (100 feet).

Third pitch variation, Guides Wall

3a. Climb a long, left-facing dihedral on the left side of the arête and belay at a stance at its top (100 feet). **3b.** From the trees, move right along the ledge and belay at two boulders. Climb a steep finger crack with pitons to a ledge (8), pull over a roof (7), and continue up easier terrain to a ledge with a small tree (100 feet).

4. From either option on pitch three, climb a short, easy pitch to Flake Ledge, a long terrace that wraps around the arête and is characterized by a 30-foot spike of rock.

5a. Climb twin cracks just right of the spike (7) and belay at a stance just past the roof (80 feet). **5b.** Climb the exquisite hand crack a few feet to the right and merge left at the roof (9+). One may also crank through the roof at an obvious spike (10b/c). **5c.** Begin to the left of the spike and tackle a right-facing flake/crack (10c).

6. Continue up a shallow dihedral and a thin crack with three fixed pins (8+), move left on a ledge and belay from a two-bolt anchor. Rappel.

Descent. Only the first six pitches of the route are described. The upper 34 pitches are seldom climbed and would likely cause one to miss the six o'clock boat. Make the first of four long rappels from the bolt anchor at the top of the sixth pitch. Note that the second and third rappels are from trees and that a short traverse southward along a ledge is required to reach the final bolt anchor, 150 feet above the start of the climb.

Baxter's Pinnacle – South Ridge
Grade II 8

THERE ARE VERY FEW "short subjects" in the Tetons – that is, compact rock climbs with easy access – and among such leisurely outings, Baxter's Pinnacle is as short as they come. A 30-minute approach leads to several pitches of good rock with a sunny southern exposure and pleasant vista above Jenny Lake. The pinnacle can be seen – with difficulty – from the Jenny Lake visitor area, low on the southeast slope of the long east ridge that descends from Symmetry Spire. The south face of the summit tower first was climbed on June 26, 1947 by Alfred Baxter and Ulf Ramm-Erickson; it first was free-climbed by John Gill during August of 1957. The entire South Ridge route as described below was first climbed by Barry Corbet and Robert French on July 27, 1958.

Approach. Take the boat across Jenny Lake or walk around as described above. In either case, from a trail junction a short way north of the boat landing, take the "horse trail" up Cascade Canyon. After about a half mile, Baxter's Pinnacle can be seen on the slope to the north. Continue up the trail until just before it crosses the talus field that descends from the pinnacle. Find and ascend a footpath that leads up to the base of the south ridge.

The Route. To begin, scramble up a gully, first on the east side, then back toward the crest and belay above a large block. One also may climb in from the gully on the west side (see topo).

1. Work up and left, then back right past a tree and belay on a ledge where the terrain steepens. One also may climb straight up a steep wall with two bolts to reach the second belay (10).
2. Climb a steep crack with fixed pins to the right of the crest (8) or ascend an easier system just left of this and belay on the ridge crest.
3. Climb directly up the crest (6), finishing the pitch with a steep hand crack (6), or climb a chimney to the right (6).
4. In either case, an easy pitch brings one to the base of the intimidating summit tower. Here, the route follows a steep crack-and-corner system up and left across the south face.
5. Climb a bit to the right past a fixed pin and up to large, detached flake. Now, lieback up and left along a very steep corner with fixed pins and up double cracks to the summit.

To descend from the summit, rappel 75 feet into the notch to the north, then downclimb the steep couloir along the west side of the pinnacle. Be very careful of loose rock on the climb as well as the descent.

Mount Moran

MOUNT MORAN IS THE NORTHERN monarch of the Teton Range. Though the Grand Teton is higher and draws a good deal more attention, it cannot match the massive bulk and complexity of this awesome peak. Rising from the shores of both Leigh and Jackson Lakes, its 12,605-foot summit presents an elevation gain of some 5800 feet – a respectable day's jaunt by any standard. That the peak sees relatively few ascents is due not only to its lesser height, but also because no maintained trail leads to any of its routes. The earliest-known attempt on the summit was made by LeRoy Jeffers, who, on August 11, 1919, climbed the Skillet Glacier to the false summit of the northeast ridge. He no doubt would have continued to the main summit, but was turned back by darkness and bad weather. He returned to the peak on August 6, 1922 with W.H. Loyster, but upon reaching the main summit, found evidence that the peak had been climb via the same route just ten days earlier by L.H. Hardy, Ben C. Rich and Bennet McNulty.

The sprawling ramparts of Mount Moran are sufficiently complex as to render a verbal description both protracted and bewildering. Fortunately, the three routes cataloged here ascend adjacent aspects of the mountain and begin from nearly the same point along the shore of Leigh Lake. Thus, our survey of terrain features may be kept thankfully brief. Viewing the mountain from the southeast, it is useful to identify the following features: The West Horn (left) and East Horn are the two large towers on either side of the Falling Ice Glacier. Rising above the glacier is the 1,000-foot CMC Face, with the conspicuous Black Dike leading to the summit. Just west of the West Horn, and rather difficult to see from a distance, is a smaller tower called Drizzlepuss. Hidden behind it and to the northwest is a still smaller

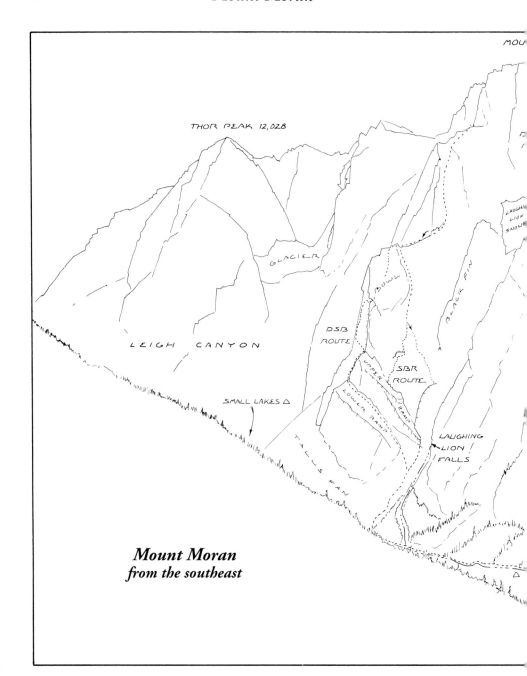

MOU

THOR PEAK 12,028

GLACIER

LAUGHI
LION
SNOW

BOWL

LEIGH CANYON

DSB
ROUTE

BLACK FIN

SMALL LAKES △

UPPER RAMP

SBR
ROUTE

LOWER RAMP

TALUS FAN

LAUGHING
LION
FALLS

△

Mount Moran
from the southeast

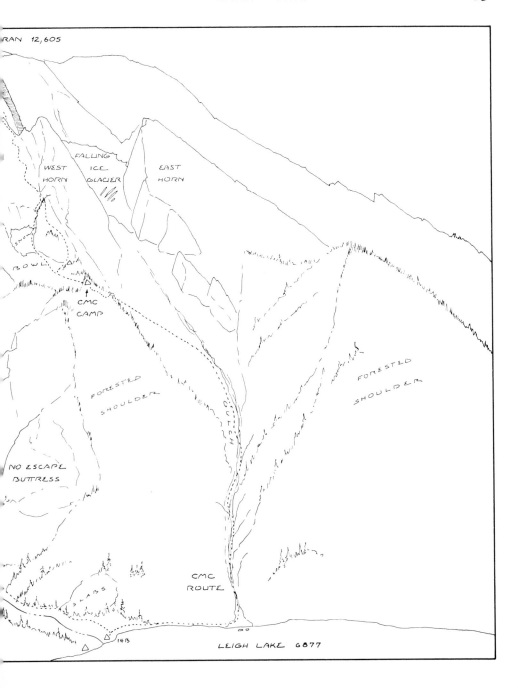

tower called Unsoeld's Needle. The massive wall of rock down to the south that towers above Leigh Canyon is the South Buttress. Immediately southwest of Mount Moran and connected to it by a high ridge is Thor Peak (12,028 ft.).

Approach. The easiest way to reach Mount Moran is by canoe. If this mode of travel is ruled out, begin at the String Lake Picnic area, shoulder thy burden, and hike the Valley Trail to the north end of Leigh Lake. From here, labor westward along a primitive trail that follows the shoreline to the cascade that descends from the Falling Ice Glacier. A good campsite lies a short way further along the shore at the mouth of Leigh Canyon. This area also may be reached via a nasty bushwhack along the southwest shore of Leigh Lake.

To proceed via canoe, make the initial launch at the String Lake picnic area and paddle to the north end of the lake, where a sign marks the beginning of a 300-yard portage to Leigh Lake. The mouth of Leigh Canyon is at the extreme west end of Leigh Lake. The entire approach via canoe requires about 90 minutes. The ascent, including approach, usually is made in two days. Make camp at any of three sites near the mouth of Leigh Canyon.

Descent. To descend from the summit, one simply may reverse the CMC ROUTE. However, the most expedient downclimb does not follow the usual line of ascent. Begin about 50 feet south of the Black Dike, and scramble down toward the West Horn via ramps and ledges. After about 300 feet, traverse south across the top of a deep gully and continue down and south to the very edge of the CMC face. Note that a rappel route begins about 400 feet beneath the summit plateau, about midway between the deep gully and south edge of the face. Two ropes are required for this rappel. From the south edge of the face, move around into a large south-facing corner system and descend another 300 feet or so until it is easy to work back left to a rappel station on the edge of the face. Rappel 165 feet or downclimb (5) the slab to the left (north) of Unsoeld's Needle, to an area of sloping ledges. Descend another 100 feet and make a 150-foot horizontal traverse to a small ledge at the southeast corner of the Needle. Rappel 50 feet into the narrow notch immediately west of Drizzlepuss, or downclimb into the notch via a steep dihedral (4).

From here, it is necessary to climb the vertical but ledgey west face of Drizzlepuss. From the notch, descend about 20 feet to the south, then work up and right (4) along a ledge that leads out across the west face. At the first opportunity, move up to the next ledge, whence it is possible to continue more easily to the top of the tower.

As an alternative, one can descend southward from the notch about 50 feet to an easier ledge that angles out into the middle of the face, then work up and left to join the other line. Depending on the skill of the climbing party, it may be advisable (on ascent) to leave an extra rope in a rappel anchor about half-way up the west face so that the initial moves out of the notch (7 – straight up) can be toproped on return from the summit.

From the top of Drizzlepuss, scramble southeast down snow or scree to some cairns on a shoulder topped with scrub trees. The shoulder is to the south of the West Horn. The simplest route from here is to descend a broad gully to the south and east on snow or talus, until the conspicuous wooded ridge of the CMC camp is reached. It also is

West face of the Drizzlepuss

possible, though more difficult, to reach the camp by scrambling down a steep and erratic path that leads more easterly from the cairns. This option is not recommended unless it also was the path of ascent. From the CMC camp, follow a distinct path down to the east, then north, to gain the drainage beneath the Falling Ice Glacier. The drainage leads, without significant obstruction, to the shore of Leigh Lake.

CMC Route

Grade II 4 to 6

THIS DIRECT LINE ON THE SOUTHEAST aspect of the mountain is the most popular summit route and is the route most often used for descent. Not ironically then, its first ascent by Paul Petzolt, Joseph Hawkes, Earl Clark and Harold Plumely of the Chicago Mountaineering Club, came six years after it first was descended by Chris Scoredos and Joe Merhar on July 14, 1935. The latter two had made the second ascent of the South Ridge. The CMC ROUTE features minimal bushwhacking, sound rock, tremendous relief and a splendid campsite with water at about 10,000 feet. The entire ascent may be managed unroped by a competent cragster but bear in mind that some steep and tricky downclimbing is required. Most parties will want to belay and rappel the steeper sections of the route. This is a very long climb and one can get a jump on the ascent by hiking up to the CMC camp the day before going to the summit.

The Route. Begin the ascent at the rocky stream gully that leads to the Falling Ice Glacier. Switch banks as needed and follow the stream to about the 9,000-foot level. Contour around to the southwest for some 200 yards and pick up a distinct trail that climbs a steep, grassy slope onto a wooded ridge. After a few switchbacks, the trail leads straight up the ridge to the CMC camp at 10,000 feet. This site is identified easily by four or five man-made enclosures clustered in a narrow stand of pine trees. Water may be found in the boulderfield about 100 feet to south.

The next objective is to reach the summit of Drizzlepuss. Perhaps the easiest of two alternatives is to hike west-northwest up the broad, open gully directly above the spring at the CMC camp. This typically will require the use of mountain boots and an ice axe – at least until August. Bear right near the top of the cirque and pick up a faint trail that leads to the talus field below the West Horn. Note that there is a cairn near the highest trees on the right (east). Hike northwest to the col between the West Horn and Drizzlepuss, then scramble without difficulty to the summit of the latter. In early to mid-season, one may avoid the snow gully by hiking directly up the ridge above the CMC camp to a bench with a few more tent enclosures. Climb an easy chimney through the cliffband above the bench and pick up a faint path that meanders up the steep, wooded ridge above and north of the gully. With careful navigation, this will bring one to the cairn at the highest trees just south of the West Horn.

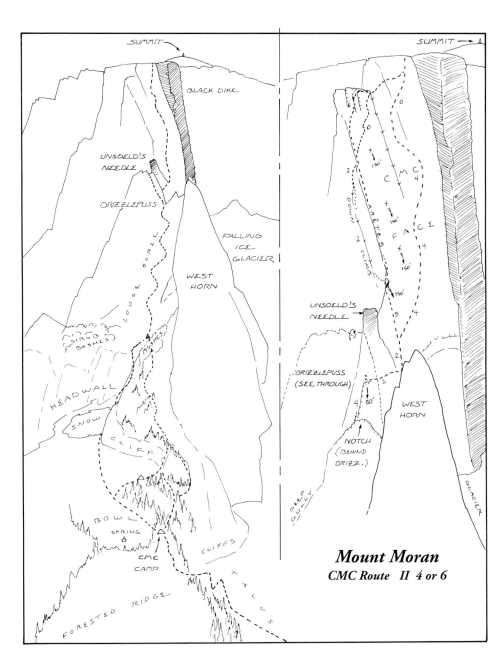

SUMMIT

BLACK DIKE

UNSOELD'S
NEEDLE

DRIZZLEPUSS

FALLING
ICE
GLACIER

LOOSE SCREE

WEST
HORN

BUSHES

SCRUB
BUSHES

HEADWALL

SNOW

CLIFF

BOWL

SPRING

CMC
CAMP

CLIFFS

TALUS

FORESTED RIDGE

SUMMIT →

CMC FACE

DOWN CLIMB

ARETES

150'

150'

150'

150'

UNSOELD'S
NEEDLE

DRIZZLEPUSS
(SEE THROUGH)

4 50'

WEST
HORN

NOTCH
(BEHIND
DRIZZ.)

DEEP GULLY

GLACIER

Mount Moran
CMC Route   II 4 or 6

From the summit of Drizzlepuss, the CMC Face comes into full view, and there is an opportunity to examine the upper 1,000 feet of the route. The narrow spire just across the gap to the west is Unsoeld's Needle. Downclimb (4) or rappel the steep west face of Drizzlepuss into the narrow notch at its base. Rope up. Ascend a left-facing dihedral on Unsoeld's Needle for about 50 feet (4) to a piton anchor, then make a 150-foot horizontal traverse to the right, out onto the CMC Face. Work up and left for about 100 feet toward the notch above the Needle, then take the line of least resistance up the headwall, staying well left of the black dike, to the summit plateau (see topo). The true summit is the huge mound of shattered sandstone (!) a short way to the north from the top of the Black Dike.

Arête Variation (6). A more difficult, and perhaps more aesthetic, variation continues up and left past Unsoeld's Needle to the arête at the left edge of the face (5). Follow the clean, exposed arête for several long pitches to near its very top (6), then traverse right for a couple of hundred feet and climb a short, steep dihedral with good protection (6). Continue to the right across the top of a deep gully (see descent), then work up the final slabs and ledges as with the regular route.

South Buttress Right
Grade IV   11a

FROM THE EASTERN SHORE OF LEIGH LAKE, the great south buttress of Mount Moran appears on the left in profile against Thor Peak. This dramatic rampart rises steeply out of Leigh Canyon for more than 1,500 feet to reach a level section, then continues as a jagged ridge for another 3,000 feet to the summit. Find here two routes of great renown. The nearly vertical western prow of the buttress is ascended by the DIRECT SOUTH BUTTRESS route, which also follows the long upper ridge to the summit. About 500 feet down to the east, across the broad south face of the buttress, a series of huge right-facing dihedrals and overhangs angle up and right in dramatic stages to merge with the upper ridge. Here lies what many consider to be the finest rock climb in all the Tetons – the SOUTH BUTTRESS RIGHT. This route ascends a narrow section of face that literally hangs in space between two immense corner-and-roof systems. The rock is extremely fine-grained and solid, and the exposure is breathtaking. One has the option to connect with the DIRECT SOUTH BUTTRESS route and vie for the summit, or to rappel after the first eight pitches.

Rack up to a #3 Friend or equivalent, with relatively few RPs and stoppers. Two of the smallest TCUs or 1/4-inch pitons can be used at the crux (pitch three). The route first was climbed on July 25, 1961 by Dave Dornan and Herb Swedlund. The first complete free ascent of the original line was made on August 2, 1978 by Buck Tilley and Jim Mullin.

Approach. Reach the designated campsites at the mouth of Leigh Canyon as described for the CMC ROUTE. Camp here, or proceed approximately a half-mile up the canyon – to a point directly south of the west arête of No Return Buttress – and find a good campsite in a stand of trees on the south side of the stream. There are several paths leading out of the lakeside campsites, and taking the wrong one in the wee hours of

South Buttress Right, pitch six

the morning would be a disastrous affair, as lower Leigh Canyon is a maze of fallen trees, bogs and dense undergrowth. The correct path begins at the edge of campsite 14b and to the northeast of the fire grate. After a few feet, a right branch leads along the lake to the CMC ROUTE, so bear left. The path is sinuous and sometimes indistinct, but for the most part, stays in the bottom of the valley, always on the north side of the stream.

After about three-quarters of a mile, the path fades and one breaks out of the woods. Continue along the bank of the stream until below a gully that descends from a waterfall up on the peak. Note that this is the last point along the approach from which the route can be examined. The unlikely water course is called Laughing Lion Falls. The compelling, narrow arête to the right is the Staircase Arête; to the left of the falls is the massive south buttress. The "Direct" lies just beyond the prow on the western skyline. The hanging plane of the SOUTH BUTTRESS RIGHT is discernable about midway between the prow and Laughing Lion Falls. Note also the two long ramps that angle up to the west across the bottom of the buttress. Scramble up the talus slope just left of the gully to the highest ledge just left of the falls and rope up.

The Route. Climb a grungy chimney (8) or a clean crack to the right (9; 4 inches), then a short right-facing corner (60 feet). This brings one to the east end of the upper of the two long ramps. Now, unrope and scramble up the ramp for about 600 feet to the bottom of a right-facing dihedral system, which may be identified by a large boulder at left and a pointed block about 15 feet up a small dihedral. There are three options for starting the route.

1a. Climb a shallow left-facing corner and crack (7) about 30 feet east of the boulder. **1b.** Climb a finger crack in a right-facing dihedral (9) about 20 feet east of the boulder. **1c.** Climb the face directly above the boulder (8) and move right around the pointed block to gain the corner system. All versions merge and lead to a belay ledge via an easy crack (90 feet). Beware of some exfoliation about halfway up.

2. Climb a right-facing dihedral with a tricky lieback (9), then jam an easy crack on the right to a large ramp that slopes down to the east (100 feet).

3. Work up into a large right-facing dihedral with some fixed pins, make a desperate undercling out to the right (11a; smallest TCUs), and crank around the corner to a "thank God" fixed pin. Lieback up the dihedral to a stance with a bolt (10b/c; optional belay), and finish with a thin crack (9; three pins) that leads to a sloping belay ledge (100 feet).

4. Climb a left-facing corner and roof just above the belay to a ledge (8), go up and right past a flake, then move right via an easy hand traverse to an exposed, marginal stance at the near side of a right-facing corner (100 feet). Before the hand traverse, a tempting crack goes straight up to what appears to be another ledge; this is off-route.

5. To the east of the right-facing dihedral, one no doubt will have already noticed an immense, hanging slab. There are some narrow ledges at the far side. Your mission, should you choose to accept it, is to reach the ledges and traverse east to

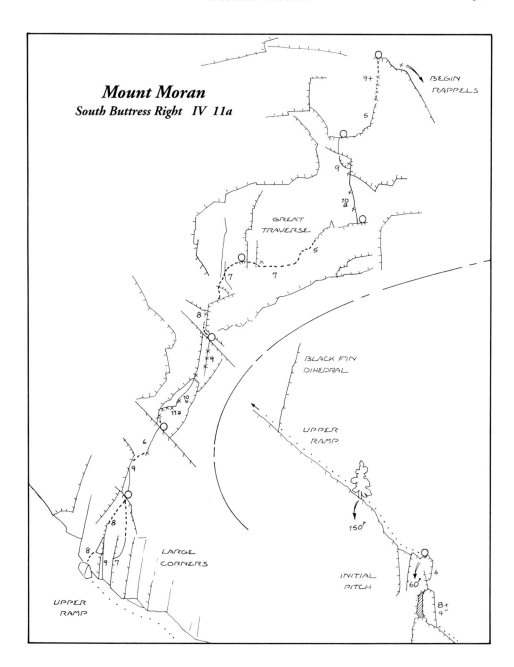

Mount Moran
South Buttress Right IV 11a

BEGIN
RAPPELS

9+

5

9

10
a

GREAT
TRAVERSE

5

7   7

8

BLACK FIN
DIHEDRAL

9

10
b

11a

UPPER
RAMP

6

9

150'

8

8   9 7

LARGE
CORNERS

INITIAL
PITCH

6

60'

UPPER
RAMP

8+
4"

where they end. This is the Great Traverse – a most dramatic pitch. Move right past the dihedral to a fixed pin (one also may sling a horn about 25 feet above the pin), continue almost straight right on small scoops and edges (no protection), and gain a series of flakes that lead up to the ledges (7). Belay at the far right beneath an obvious, left-angling hand crack (150 feet).

6. Lieback and jam the crack (10a), work up and left through a V- shaped break in the roof (9), and belay on a large, grassy ledge (150 feet).

7. Move the belay to the east end of the ledge. Climb a left-facing flake/corner, and the smooth face above past four antique bolts (9+, 90 feet).

Descent. A cluster of slings 25 feet down to the east marks the beginning of the rappel route back to the start of the climb, by Laughing Lion Falls (see topo of descent). One also may do several more nice pitches up and left to join the DIRECT SOUTH BUTTRESS route at the long, level stretch in the ridge.

Direct South Buttress
Grade IV   7 A3 or 12a

IN EVERY MOUNTAIN RANGE, there are a few routes that, due to their length, position, quality and history, are recognized by climbers as the great classic lines. The DIRECT SOUTH BUTTRESS on Mount Moran is a route of such stature, and at the time of its first ascent, was the hardest in the Tetons. The "Direct" combines difficult aid and free climbing on the very prow of the south buttress, then continues – more easily – up the long, rugged south ridge to the summit. The route first was climbed on August 29 and 30, 1953 by Richard Emerson, Don Decker and Leigh Ortenburger.

Approach. Proceed as for SOUTH BUTTRESS RIGHT all the way to the talus slope beneath Laughing Lion Falls (see above). Viewed from this position, the route lies just beyond the skyline of the sheer, western prow of the buttress. Note that two prominent ramps cut up and left (westward) toward the prow. Reach the beginning of the route by scrambling all the way to the top of the lower ramp. Camp as described for South Buttress Right or at a small lake about 1.5 miles up Leigh Canyon. One also may bivouac near the top of the lower ramp. Rack up to a #4 Friend or equivalent.

The Route. Rope up about 50 feet around to the left from the top of the ramp, between two trees.

1 **and 2.** Climb a chimney system for 200 feet and belay at the top of the upper ramp (0).

3. Move the belay about 50 feet to the west. Work up and right, then back left to a long ledge system that curves up to the left (7).

4. Scramble up and left along the ledge for 165 feet (4).

5. Climb up and left past fixed pins and belay on a ramp (8).

6. From the ramp, climb up and right past a flake, then straight up the right-facing dihedral to a roof. Hand traverse left (9) and belay at a large flake. Note that there are easier alternatives to these pitches to the left (see topo).

Pitch nine, Direct South Buttress
Paul Gagner photo

7. Climb a left-facing dihedral, then work up the clean chimney formed by the long, detached flake and belay at its top (7).

8. Climb up to the left side of a huge, white-topped flake, lieback up around its left side, then work up past a thin, pointed flake to a ledge (7).

9. Work up and right to a ledge with a fixed pin, move to the right around a blunt arête, and climb a steep crack up to a tiny ledge beneath two bolts (8).

10. This is the famous double-pendulum pitch. Climb up to the bolts, lower 20 feet, then pendulum to a wafer piton. Lower down again, and swing across to a

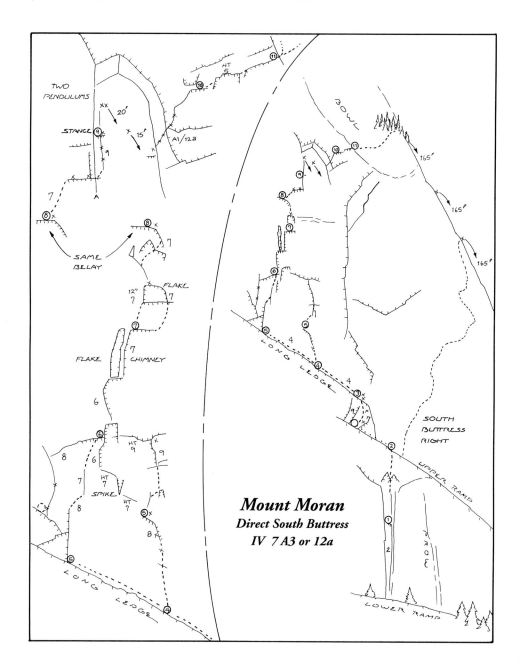

Mount Moran
Direct South Buttress
IV 7 A3 or 12a

small stance below a thin crack (one can belay here). Aid (A1) or free climb (12a) up and right past fixed pins to a good ledge and belay. The pendulum can be free climbed straight across at 11d.

11. Hand traverse to the right along a good flake and, after about 100 feet, belay on a ledge at the bottom of a huge basin or bowl (5). If a bivouac is required, scramble up and right into the bowl to an area of small pine trees. Water may be found here in early to mid season.

To continue to the summit, climb along the left edge of the basin, gain the crest of the south ridge, and traverse a level section for 1,000 feet to the next steep step in the ridge. There are several pinnacles along this section, the last of which may require a 60-foot rappel. Pass a notch (see descent), traverse a bit to the right and ascend the ridge, staying mostly on the east side of the crest. The final steep section before the summit is most easily negotiated on the west side. The entire ridge above the south buttress can be climbed unroped by a competent team, and if the easiest line is found, the difficulty does not exceed 4. Use the CMC ROUTE to descend from the summit (see above).

Descent. To avoid the upper 3,000 feet of the south ridge and return to Leigh Canyon, scramble up to the notch at the north end of the level section of the south ridge as described above. From here, two steep gullies divided by a rock rib drop down to the west. Downclimb the left gully for about 250 feet, then change to the right (more northerly) gully and follow it down into the basin between Thor Peak and the south ridge. This is no piece of cake, but can be downclimbed without rappels. An alternate descent, with more rappeling and less downclimbing, can be made to the east from the trees, up and right across the basin from the top of the eleventh pitch. From the lowest of these trees, make two long rappels to reach the top of the rappel for SOUTH BUTTRESS RIGHT (see topo on the following page).

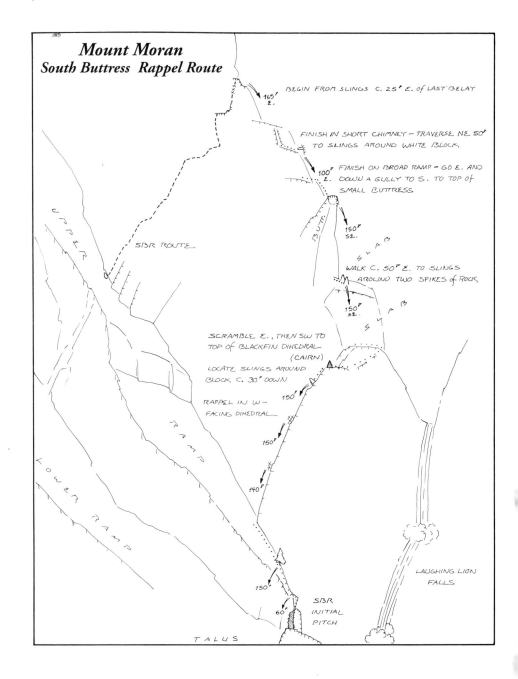

Mount Moran
South Buttress Rappel Route

BEGIN FROM SLINGS C. 25° E. of LAST BELAY

165'
E.

FINISH IN SHORT CHIMNEY — TRAVERSE NE 50'
TO SLINGS AROUND WHITE BLOCK

100'
E.

FINISH ON BROAD RAMP — GO E. AND
DOWN A GULLY TO S. TO TOP OF
SMALL BUTTRESS

SBR ROUTE

150'
SE.

SLAB

WALK C. 50° E. TO SLINGS
AROUND TWO SPIKES of ROCK

150'
SE.

UPPER

SCRAMBLE E., THEN SW TO
TOP OF BLACKFIN DIHEDRAL
(CAIRN)

LOCATE SLINGS AROUND
BLOCK C. 30' DOWN

150'

RAPPEL IN W—
FACING DIHEDRAL

150'

140'

RAMP

LOWER RAMP

LAUGHING LION
FALLS

150'

60'   SBR
      INITIAL
      PITCH

TALUS